Better Than I Should Be

Overcoming Sexual and Domestic Abuse through Forgiveness and Personal Healing

Christina Warren Ivey

Trilogy Christian Publishers

A Wholly Owned Subsidiary of Trinity Broadcasting Network

2442 Michelle Drive

Tustin, CA 92780

Copyright © 2023 by Christina Warren Ivey

All rights reserved, including the right to reproduce this book or portions thereof in any form whatsoever.

Scripture quotations marked (KJV) taken from The Holy Bible, King James Version. Cambridge Edition: 1769.

For information, address Trilogy Christian Publishing

Rights Department, 2442 Michelle Drive, Tustin, CA 92780.

Trilogy Christian Publishing/TBN and colophon are trademarks of Trinity Broadcasting Network.

For information about special discounts for bulk purchases, please contact Trilogy Christian Publishing.

Manufactured in the United States of America

Trilogy Disclaimer: The views and content expressed in this book are those of the author and may not necessarily reflect the views and doctrine of Trilogy Christian Publishing or the Trinity Broadcasting Network.

10 9 8 7 6 5 4 3 2 1

Library of Congress Cataloging-in-Publication Data is available.

ISBN 979-8-89041-450-2

ISBN (ebook) 979-8-89041-451-9

TABLE OF CONTENTS

FOREWORD 5

INTRODUCTION 9

BETRAYED 13

FAMILY SECRETS 19

LIFE DEPOSITS 25

TEENAGE LOVE 35

TAKING ADVANTAGE 43

GLIMPSE OF HOPE 51

BACK TO REALITY 61

I TRIED, NOW I'M DONE 69

1995 - PART I 77

1995 - PART II 95

SECOND TIME AROUND 107

NOT AGAIN 115

ON SECOND THOUGHT 119

GIVE ME A BREAK 133

INDISCRETION 143

WORK IT OUT 149

UNEXPECTED 155

FORGIVENESS 161

TIME VERSUS WOUNDS 165

LOVE ME 167

GOING FORWARD 169

ACKNOWLEDGMENTS 173

FOREWORD

I vividly remember the first time I met Tina. It was a warm summer day and we stopped to get gas at the hangout/gas station affectionately deemed "Earnie's," which was located in the middle of the tiny new town my husband and I now called *home*. A black pickup truck pulled up and stopped across the lot from us and out popped a curly haired, well-built teenager who was all smiles. My husband, Chap, introduced her as "Tina, one of our youth." What a huge understatement that would come to be!

No time was wasted getting to know most of the people in this small town of merely 1700 residents, where everyone seemed to know everyone. Church life was a way of life for most of the families in this Bible belt region of North Carolina. The first close friendship I developed was with that curly haired tomboy who frequented the gas station on the weekends, and soon we were together several days per week. We weren't a likely pair, complete opposites to be precise, but we were most definitely a match made in Heaven and by God's design! Trust evolved quickly and conversations flowed with ease, both of which are surprising, given what this young, beautiful girl had been through in her short 19 years. Although we were fast friends, it often felt that she was holding something back, like she wanted to share something more but just couldn't bring herself to do so.

Over time, I began to notice Tina would become withdrawn when I mentioned her family, especially her dad. My once bubbly, fun-loving friend was moody; she often complained of physical pain and issues that would result in her not participating in her much-loved sporting events and church outings. It wasn't until she and I were traveling back from Virginia one evening that she confided in me only part of her story.

Slowly but surely over the years, the entire story emerged, and more than ever I wanted to be the friend who stood by her unconditionally and to see her be completely healed of this trauma. I pressed gently but relentlessly for Tina to share all of her story so the people who loved her (myself at the top of that list) could better understand and help her. I believed that one day she may even be able to help others who have faced this grueling situation. That is exactly what she has done in this memoir of her life story. For years, I sought to be her "go to," her "ride or die" and most of all, her mentor. As God would have it and ironically enough, the opposite

FOREWORD

is true. She is the strong one. The teacher. The mentor. No one will know the courage, stress, anxiety, revisited trauma and so many other emotions she endured to share her story. There were those who didn't believe her, those who blamed her, and those who just couldn't accept this truth. Now, with the help of her Lord, she shares with her readers the story of innocence stolen, growth, and healing. I couldn't be prouder of MY mentor.

Your friend,

Kris Chappell

INTRODUCTION

Has there ever been a time you felt you were floating mindlessly through life with no real direction? As I was dragging into the thirty-something chapter of my life, it was as if life was dictating everything about me. My existence revolved around pleasing everyone, except the One I should have been pleasing. The word "No" was not in my vocabulary, not to the physical person anyway. But when it came to God that one little word was the biggest word I never verbally spoke, yet my actions said loud and clear. Until one day…I was invited to get reacquainted with God on a more personal level. That was the day I answered God with a resounding "YES!"

Looking back, I can see God's hand in everything. Through all my accomplishments to my most devastating failure, God was building me up to step across the line in the sand and into the destiny He had prepared for me. My life has not been the best and I've made my share of mistakes, but I have learned from those mistakes. I've also learned through adversity not created by my own selfish decisions or through my sometimes ignorant, self-inflicted emotional wounds. Through all of the sexual abuse, peer pressure, depression, and just plain stubbornness, I can honestly say I know God has a purpose for my life.

Sometimes I pride myself in my stubbornness. Many times, well, most of the time if I'm honest, I find myself thinking I can do this—life, that is—on my own. That is how my logic works, but my spirit does not agree with my reasoning. I have been independent for so long, it has been difficult to trust God to do what only He can do. I could say God has been holding me at a level beneath my potential. But the truth is, it is not God who is holding me back. He has been waiting for me to be obedient. My failure to walk in obedience, usually through procrastination, has been my downfall. My stubbornness and rebelliousness are my restrainers, not God. He wants to see me striving for and walking out the victory He has already given me. Knowing what God requires of me, I can no longer make excuses. I once heard someone say, "There are people on the other side of your obedience who need what you have to offer." So as long as I procrastinate, I am no good to the Kingdom of God. This may be my life, but it was never meant for me alone. We exist for each other. I must carry out His assignment for me. And that assignment is to encourage others who have had similar life-altering experiences and tell them there is hope, and that Hope is Jesus.

INTRODUCTION

"Which hope we have as an anchor of the soul, both sure and steadfast, and which entereth into that within the veil."

— Hebrews 6:19 (KJV)

BETRAYED

"All right, are you ready?" I heard that dreaded voice call from behind my closed door.

"Yeah, I'm up," I sleepily moaned. My mind was warring against the action I had to take. It was time to drive him to work again. [*God, please let him go straight to work today.*] I reluctantly got up, already dressed in my sweats and a t-shirt. I grabbed my shoes and the biggest jacket I could find, the jacket offering only false security from what I prayed wouldn't happen again. Out the door we went.

The drive, on any normal trip, would last only six or seven minutes. On those dreadful days, the ones where I longed to be anywhere but there, they lasted an agonizing lifetime in my mind. The four-mile trip just down the road seemed like a cross-country road trip to hell. Not many people traveled the narrow dirt road, let alone noticed when he would turn into the overgrown path traveling toward my worst nightmare. My mind wandered, trying to escape what my body was about to endure.

A poor excuse for small talk didn't hide what he was undeniably thinking. There were many ways to show someone you love them, but this was absolutely horrendous. What made someone act this way? Of course, he said he loved me, but didn't he know the difference? This wasn't the kind of affection to be shared between anyone but a husband and wife. What was he thinking?

The next twenty minutes were spent with me wishing I were either dead, a million miles away, or someone else entirely. If I screamed, no one would hear me. If I resisted, he would make life miserable for everyone, not just me. If I ran, where would I go without causing the drama that would surely follow? What would people say?

"She's a liar."

"She instigated it."

"I heard he went to prison because she lied on him before."

What would my family say? My mom? And what about my classmates? I already felt like people treated me differently, because in my mind everybody knew my past. In my mind, what could be worse than rejection and humiliation? The only choice I saw was to endure the pain myself. It sounded a little masochistic, but I would rather inflict pain upon myself than anyone else. My hands were tied. I couldn't see any way out.

After I took my father to work, I headed home feeling dirty and shameful. I cried as I drove the four-mile return trip. The tears weren't just of hurt; they were more than that. They were tears of hatred, disgust, and utter betrayal. The tears were not directed at the object of my affliction, but at myself! I hated what I let him do to me. I was disgusted by what he did, but more at the fact I didn't stop him. And betrayal…he may have betrayed my trust, but I betrayed myself more by not protecting myself.

Quit your cryin' and get it together. Someone is gonna see you, I thought. *Okay, Tina, pull yourself together.* I walked through the front door. The first place I headed was to the shower.

And so began another typical day in my life. Another day of playing charades and hiding what was happening.

Reflection

"Why?" is the question I have always pondered, though I am not sure I want to know how someone could have such thoughts, or better yet, do what he did. Children do not provoke or ask to be molested or raped/assaulted. How could someone say they love you and then subject you to so much hell? God never intended for it to be this way. What happened to protecting children? They are not property to do with as one pleases. God entrusts them into the care of their parents. Children are gifts and should be treasured, not betrayed.

Much of an adult's character is built on the foundation of their childhood. A stable childhood helps create stronger character, which enables the child to explore who they are without fear. Knowing someone is there to help when they don't know which way to go is comforting in and of itself.

Then there are those like me, who struggled to do the right things. Those who wished they had a normal childhood, absent from abuse, wanting to feel accepted for who they are, not as a charity case, wondering why the lessons they learned were the ones taught. No one in their right mind would want to be in that class. I know I never did. Who wants to feel so ashamed they would rather die? Who wants to cry themselves to sleep and dream they can get away, only to wake up and realize it was just that…a dream? Who prays someone will open their eyes and see what is going on? We all do. I know I did.

The sad fact is many children of abuse will never make it out. In untold cases, no one cares enough to help change the situation and others prefer not to get involved.

BETRAYED

Oftentimes, the child is seen as a liar and the family treats them as an outsider. These are only a few of the reasons childhood sexual abuse remains hidden. The victims want to be spared the shame of their abuse and the looks of disbelief, disgust, and judgment that accompany the knowledge of it. Knowing how to read the signs and how to ask the questions is key in preventing and/or stopping this atrocity. Learn how you can help. Offer solutions. You may be the answer to their prayers.

FAMILY SECRETS

An unfamiliar lady sat on our couch as I walked in the door of our double-wide mobile home. My mom stood by with a look of horror on her tear-stained face. Then I noticed more people staring in my direction. None of their faces were familiar to me. Why were they here, and why were they looking at me?

I soon found out.

Our uninvited guests had me sit down to ask me questions. I was not sure what they were expecting by talking to me; I was a child. What would a nine-year-old possibly know that was so important?

I quickly realized the secret was out! He told me not to tell, and I didn't. Somehow, these people knew and they didn't look happy at all. I saw the pain on my mom's face as she continued to cry during my interview with the social worker. I was worried I would be in trouble. My mind raced. I wondered what he would do when he found out. The severity of the situation became evident when they informed us he could not be around me until they had more answers. As I stared out the living room window, I questioned if I would be taken away in that police car. I didn't want to be in trouble. As the questions continued, my mind replayed a recent incident...

Like they often did, my grandmother and mother were leaving for the evening to drive my uncle to his college classes. This meant they would be gone for several hours, and for me, that meant disaster. My brother Tom, who was just under two years older than me, and I would be left at home with our dad. My brother's presence, however, would not stop what would inevitably happen. Tom would be sent outside to play, while I became my father's center of attention. Once Tom was preoccupied, my dad would send me to his room and instruct me on what he expected. I did as I was told, and despite my age and innocence, I still felt that this was not right. Otherwise, why would he demand me not to tell?

But someone found out.

Reflection

Like most people, I have good memories of my childhood. One of those memories is going to the drive-in theater and the smell of the smoking green circular insect repellant that sat on the dash next to the movie speaker, which hung just outside of the truck window. It's the little things that stick in our memories. Those were good times. However, most of the good memories are clouded by the bad. I've been through hell and back, more than anyone should have to endure. It's only by the grace of God that I am the person I am today. From the very beginning, God has had His hand on me. I see that in how He saved me; how He hand-picked those who would befriend me, mentor me, and encourage me to never give up; and by how He sustained me through all of my wrong decisions. With all that I have been through, I would be a societal wreck if not for His grace and mercy. My past may be a statistic, but my outcome far outweighs the odds.

I remember as a very young child going to church with our neighbor. That is where I gained my spiritual foundation. Only God knew at that point how important it would be for me to learn about Him at an early age. While I was having fun meeting new friends and playing games, He was shaping who I would become. Now I see how He was working even then.

I had a lot of fun at church. Although in other parts of my life, fun was definitely not what I was having. One of the worst things imaginable was happening behind closed doors. Being young and innocent, I had no idea how to deal with the abuse I faced or how it would affect who I would be and what I would experience as an adult.

The one thing I did know was the fear of someone finding out the family secret, especially my mom. For a long time, that's exactly how things were. The secret was safe…but I wasn't.

My mom was in the dark, and my brother was always sent out to play. I'm really not sure if my brother knew what was going on or if he too had to carry a secret. But I can tell you it caused a strained relationship between us. From the outside, my family was your average working-class family that was active in the community. We weren't rich, but we weren't lacking either. That would all change when the actual truth came out. That's when everything I'd ever known was altered forever, and my life became completely turned around. My big secret was about to be exposed.

While playing with some children in the neighborhood I must have told them about what was happening to me at home. Eventually a concerned parent reported the possible sexual abuse to the Department of Social Services. At the time I didn't realize it, but that would be one of the best things that ever happened to me.

After multiple court hearings and after several psychiatrist visits for me, my dad pleaded no contest to charges of incest and crimes against nature. He was sentenced to a little over seven years in prison. The whole time the trial was going on, I was torn between telling the social workers and attorneys what really happened and my family denying it, telling me it didn't happen. They blamed the Department of Social Services and the court for pressuring me to make up a story. The only story I gave was the one I knew, which was the truth.

LIFE DEPOSITS

After my dad was sent to prison, I was placed in foster care with a family for which I will be forever grateful.

Sounds strange, huh? Let me explain.

The family I was placed with was a God-fearing family. They were faithful in their relationship with God and it was exactly what I needed, although at the time it was not what I wanted. We went to church practically every time the doors were open. During that time, the most important event in my life happened. It was then, at nine years old, that I came to know Jesus as my Lord and Savior. So, to the family who kept me, I say, "Thank you and God bless you!"

While I was in foster care, I was able to remain in the same school. Since my foster parents' home was out of the zoning area for my school, I would ride the school bus with the high school students to the junior high school. I would then transfer to the elementary school bus for the remainder of my journey. My foster brother and sister, who rode the high school bus with me, made sure I was safe and that no one made me feel scared or threatened. My presence on that bus was awkward since it was a bus full of teenagers, although no one ever treated me disrespectfully or questioned why I was there. On one occasion, the students were daring one of them to "moon" everyone on the bus. Because I was there, the boy was apprehensive and asked another student to cover my head. One of the students then placed his coat over my head to block my view until it was over. It was these types of shenanigans the students would entertain themselves with on their way to and from school.

My friends and classmates treated me the same as always. There were no signs anyone knew the circumstances I faced. That didn't stop my mind from thinking otherwise. I felt like everyone knew my dad was in prison and that they believed it was my fault, which is not something a child should ever have to worry about.

Albeit, there was a girl who lived beside my foster family who was very judgmental and nasty to me. Her parents were well-to-do and she treated me as if I was a lesser person. Our birthdays were a few days apart, mine ten days earlier, she told me I was "ten days more rotten!" than her. This was my first encounter with being bullied. In the spring, her parents had a swimming pool installed. We would hang out and observe the army of frogs living in the massive hole in their backyard. I tried to befriend her the best I knew how under the circumstances. Not only did she say mean things to and about me, she also tried to remove my arm floaties in the deep end of the pool, knowing good and well I didn't know how to swim. I couldn't win with her.

Once the Department of Social Services thought it was safe for me to go back home, I left my foster family and my church and went back to stay with my mom and my brother. They had moved to a small two-bedroom mobile home while I was gone. When I showed up, it made the trailer seem that much smaller.

When I was back home, I had to sleep in my mom's room on the full-size bed that barely fit in the room. Otherwise, I would sleep in the tiny living room. My brother stayed in the small space where he had a twin bed that took up the majority of his room. This was home for the next six years.

I never understood how God chose which people to place in a person's life to fulfill His will. Although my life seemed really bad at the time, it led me to the first of many people who helped me in my life's journey and produced some of the greatest relationships I'd ever have. During that time, I met my childhood best friend Christa. Christa came to visit her mom, who happened to be my next-door neighbor, on the weekends. It was our relationship that would teach me what true friendship really looked like.

When Christa moved in with her mom, we spent most of our time together, playing college and just hanging out. Like most preteens, we got in our little disagreements and I went home. But fifteen minutes later it was almost like it never happened and I would be right back. At school, we did not spend very much time together. We had different classes. This influenced the social circles we would run in. Some people did not even know we were friends unless we told them. The good thing about it was even though we spent our school days in different areas and with different friends, we always knew where our friendship stood.

Christa's mom also had a big impact on my life. She took me to the church that would be my home for the next twenty plus years. It was there I regained my life in Christ that I had neglected for a few years. I began going back to church on a regular basis and became a faithful member of the girls' program in the church. It was a great help when I became depressed over the relocation of my best friend. Christa moved away and I was left with a bunch of memories and constant reminders next door. By this time, we were both facing the new pressures of going to high school and all that it entailed—relationships, extra-curricular activities, and working toward the future.

Christa and I didn't see each other very often after she moved away. I was lost once she left. Looking back, I see how she was a major asset to my transition back into my home after being with my foster family. She made coming home easier. So, it's no surprise I tried to see her as often as I could, which was very limited until I got my driver's license.

I remember one night in particular that will forever be etched in my mind. My friend Laurie and I had made plans to go out on a Friday night to the football game at Christa's high school. Once we got into town, Laurie decided to stay with her boyfriend at the stables. She allowed me to use her dad's car to go to the game. I was anxious to get there, because I hadn't seen my best friend in a long time.

I got to the game and found my friend and we watched the game until a horrible thunderstorm caught everyone off guard. The game was stopped due to the tremendous amount of lightning and hard rains. I offered Christa a ride, and before we even exited the parking lot, another girl cut in front of me and we collided. Not only was it pouring down raining and the game was cut short, but now I'd wrecked Laurie's dad's car…that I shouldn't have been driving in the first place! But the story got even more interesting. The girl who pulled in front of me was there from the next county over and was there without her parents' permission. So, we both freaked out. We couldn't reach my friend Laurie for quite some time, but when we did we learned that she had some drama of her own. She and her boyfriend had broken up, and she had to tell her dad I wrecked his car. Thankfully no one received a citation and each vehicle owner was responsible for their own vehicle's repairs.

Once we returned back to Laurie's house and she broke the news to her dad, the worst part was over. He was not pleased by any means, but grateful the damage was minimal. I personally did not have any repercussions from the accident, but Laurie may not have been so lucky. What a disastrous night!

Over the years Christa and I grew apart, but there was a mutual knowledge that if we needed anything, we could count on each other. The same is true today and I thank God for her friendship.

LIFE DEPOSITS

Reflection

Adolescence. What a convoluted transition period from the beginning of puberty until a person comes into adulthood. So many moving parts happen all at once. Physical changes, shifts in thought patterns, new relationships, and temperament changes, just to name a few. It's the time when one begins to seek autonomy, to become their own person. It's also a time when they may still want the covering of their parent(s)/guardian. For instance, teens want to push the boundaries, until those boundaries push back, and they find themselves in a predicament. Not a child, yet not an adult. Stuck in the middle. This is such a vital time in life that it matters with whom you are stuck in the middle.

Relationships, especially friendships, are fundamental to the developmental progression into adulthood. It is with these friendships, or acquaintanceships, one finds themselves subject to the majority of the peer pressure they will face. From the brand/type of clothes they wear, to whether or not they decide to disobey their parents and partake in things they should not (drugs, alcohol, sex, partying, etc....), or possibly engaging in less-threatening activities, but still potentially injurious. However, not all peer pressure is detrimental.

Better Than I Should Be

Some peer pressure can be favorable. For example, a little coaxing from a friend could direct them into realizing a talent or passion they never knew they had. Playing a sport, learning an instrument, starting a band, painting...there are so many possibilities. Contrary to the things that can be considered as negative peer pressure, there are also equal and/or opposite things that can be said for positive peer pressure (not doing drugs or drinking, purity/abstinence, not following the crowd, creating your own style, etc....).

The difficult part about selecting friends during adolescence is that each person is navigating their own journey into adulthood. Tempers flare. Attitudes erupt. Hormones rage. Loyalties are made. Judgments are cast. Hearts are broken. Emotions are all over the place. In today's society, social media has exacerbated the lack of empathy and has promoted a sense of self-worship and vanity. Bullying has become a mainstream issue in society. Not only is it physical or verbal, now it includes cyber-bullying. This was unheard of back in the 1980s due to the lack of advanced technology we have available today. In those days, many issues were worked out in physical fights. Once a winner was established, the dispute was resolved. Very rarely did arguments end in gun violence among teens. At least it was not widely heard of in those times.

LIFE DEPOSITS

Most adults can remember, in some measure, their group of friends and the shenanigans they carried out when they were teens. Whether they look back in fondness or regret, the nostalgia of when they were young is significantly linked to the relationships they had back then. So many emotions and ideations were experienced. First loves, heartbreaks, embarrassing situations, feelings of inadequacy, arrogance, compassion, and humor are only a few attributes that are shared realities among peer groups.

I had my share of mixed emotions and a wide range of friends from all backgrounds. When I look back, I see how many of my peers affected my life. Some of my greatest memories originated during those years of my life. However, not all of those interactions were positive. But even in the unpleasant happenings, now as an adult, I can find wisdom for the present by evaluating those early life experiences.

TEENAGE LOVE

"Hey, my dad's having a party tonight. You should come over and hang out," Rachel suggested.

"I don't know if my mom will let me, but I'll ask her," I replied.

After a little begging and a lot of annoying my mom until she gave in, I was able to go to the party. Rachel's dad lived about three miles from my house and a half-mile from my grandparents' home. This played in my favor as it was close enough for someone to come get me if needed or if I needed to walk to my grandparent's house, since they were just around the corner.

Rachel pulled up in her dad's Camaro to pick me up and off we went. I was sure my mom was praying when we drove off in that sports car that we didn't act stupidly and get in an accident. Rachel knew she would be in major trouble if anything happened to her dad's car. It was his baby. So, she acted responsibly while she drove. Being free from any adults for just a few minutes, riding with the windows down and the music up, made everything right in the world, if only for the three-mile ride.

Being away from home without supervision was a

Better Than I Should Be

rare occurrence as I was usually grounded. I didn't really do much to get grounded. I had good grades and did not disrespect my elders. I did not do drugs. I was not promiscuous. My only vice was arguing with my mom about the inequality of the things my brother got to do compared to what I was permitted to do. The real truth of the situation was that my mom told my dad everything and he constantly instructed her to tell me I was grounded. Even from prison, he controlled me. But that night, I was free, at least for a little while.

Once we reached Rachel's house, we went in and spoke to all the adults as they enjoyed their adult beverages. We grabbed our sodas and snacks and headed to her dad's room to escape the adults and to watch a movie. When we walked into the room, Tommy and Kenneth were already sitting there looking for a movie to watch. I immediately recognized Tommy. We went to the same high school and had some of the same acquaintances. However, I did not know the other guy.

Rachel introduced me to Kenneth, her cousin. Kenneth was seated on a chair next to the bed and he held an electric guitar. Nothing about him immediately stood out except the fact he would not put the guitar down. It seemed odd, but if that was his thing, I thought, good for

TEENAGE LOVE

him. As for his appearance, Kenneth had a cute smile and blond hair, which was my favorite. Having recently broken up with my boyfriend Johnny, I did not give the idea of liking Kenneth any thought.

Rachel and I got comfortable on the bed and prepared to watch the film. During the movie, Rachel started laughing and pushed me off the bed. I ended up stuck between the bed and the wall and could not get up. Kenneth arose, put down his guitar, and came to my rescue. I thanked him for his quick response, and we all laughed. This broke the ice between Kenneth and me. He was quiet up until that point. Kenneth then asked me if I wanted to hold his guitar. To me, this was not that big of a deal, but it was a pretty cool guitar, I must admit.

As the night went on, the weather turned bad and it snowed. I called my mom and told her I would be home in the morning. She was not pleased, but we did not have much choice. The adults had been drinking and couldn't drive, and Rachel could not take her dad's Camaro into the snow. Just watch, I thought, once my mom told my dad, I'd be grounded AGAIN.

I made it home in the morning and my mom gave me a speech about spending the night. I gave my rebuttal, and it was back to things as normal. My mini vacay was over, if only for one night.

Rachel called to check on me and also to give me a message. "Did you get in a lot of trouble?" she asked.

"I won't know until she talks to my dad. If she tells him, I'm sure I'll be grounded."

"Hopefully you're not." Rachel stated, sounding concerned. Then she asked me what I thought about Kenneth and if I liked him.

I responded, "I think he is cute, but I didn't really think much more than that."

She told me Kenneth told her that he liked me and to ask if he could come see me. Rachel also mentioned she was surprised Kenneth let me hold his guitar because he never let anyone touch it, let alone hold it.

I agreed to see him, but I had some reservations because my mom was going to disapprove solely based on our age difference. Kenneth was 18 and I just turned 15 two weeks prior to meeting him.

Over the next few weeks, Kenneth and Tommy came to my house several days each week. Tommy was the one with the transportation, so he sat in on our visits. My mom didn't seem to mind me talking to Kenneth as long as he came to our house to see me. She kept a tight rein on me and where I went.

TEENAGE LOVE

My feelings for Kenneth came about rather quickly. I thought about him all the time and wanted to be around him. We talked about lots of things, especially about music. Music had always been an outlet for me and how I coped with all the bad things that happened in my life up to that point. Kenneth was the lead guitarist in his band, which made my attraction to him even stronger. I often went with Kenneth, Rachel, and Tommy to watch Kenneth's band practice. These were good times.

After a few months, Kenneth called with some devastating news. He had moved to the next town over with his older sister. We did not see each other as often as we once did. Kenneth had not had a stable family situation for years. This was just another move in the course of many. But it was not the move to his sister's house that was the bad news. His call was to let me know he would be moving further away to his uncle's house within the next month and we had to break up. My heart was broken. I had never felt like that over anyone, and I was losing him.

Reflection

Teenage love…what can I say? I know what some may say: that it's not real love or it's just hormones or infatuation. I can tell you that teenage love is as real as any love can get.

Do not dismiss it when someone says they are in love with another person. First of all, we cannot judge someone's feelings that only they experience. Even if we witness this same person mistreating the one they say they love, there is more to it than what you can physically see. Some people can only love as much as they have been shown love or what they view from the world, and it is not always shown how it should be.

Love is not always a reason to stay together. You can love someone and still walk away, for example, in cases of abuse. But sometimes, love is shown in marvelous ways.

Remember, God is Love, and the best way to show love is through His example, no matter if it is teenage love, mature love, or platonic love. To me, my feelings for Kenneth were an undeniable love.

For months, I thought about Kenneth all the time and

TEENAGE LOVE

I missed him like crazy. I had no way to contact him and I wasn't sure exactly where he was. (Mind you, this was way before social media and cell phones.) All I knew was the rural area he lived in. One day after I was able to drive, I made a point to try and find him. I located someone in the area with the same last name and left a note on their door for him to contact me if he lived there. I never heard a word…not back then anyway. But that was not the end of us. Be careful what you wish for.

TAKING ADVANTAGE

During the summer after my freshman year of high school, my dad returned home from prison. Per his release documentation, we could not reside in the same home. My parents sent me to live with my grandparents a few miles down the road, but that was short-lived. While I stayed with my grandparents, my dad built an extra bedroom onto the small mobile home my mom, brother, and I shared prior to his return. The extra room was needed because earlier that year my mother gave birth to my baby sister, who had been conceived while my dad was home on work-release one weekend. Having to be away from home, I felt abandoned. My brother, and now sister, were still living in the home and I was not. Though one of the positives about living with my grandparents was that I had my own room and was allowed to decorate it with all of my favorite posters: Johnny Depp, Kirk Cameron, River Phoenix, NKOTB, Debbie Gibson, and others. I was in love with Donnie Wahlberg! Haha.

My stay with my grandparents did not last. After a few short months, I experienced a horrible menstrual cycle that had me in severe pain and unable to move about. I was not a stranger to having terrible menstrual cramps, usually resulting in several missed school days each year. This time, I just wanted my mom, and to be home. I was allowed to come home with the understanding I would return to my grandparents' home once I was feeling better. Days went by. I never returned back to live with my grandparents.

With my return home, the trailer was now even smaller, as far as personal space. My dad allowed me to have the new bedroom addition, along with my younger cousin, who stayed briefly. After my cousin went back home, it wasn't long before the grooming began. My dad gave me porn magazines and porn literature to read. My mom found a magazine in my room and reprimanded me, thinking I had taken it. I didn't have them willingly; although I admit, I was a little curious about them. Things were getting problematic again. Not only did I have him pushing me to engage in looking at and reading about things I shouldn't, now I had my mom thinking I was a willing participant. Little did I know this was just the tip of the iceberg.

Eventually we moved as a whole family to the other side of town. I was also able to get my driver's license. I was so excited, but I didn't know at the time what that would later entail. Once my junior year rolled around,

TAKING ADVANTAGE

I was able to drive my dad's car to school. But in order to do so I had to first take him to work and then return home to get ready for the day. Many, if not most, of those days began with shameful acts perpetrated against me. Mentally, I was reaching a breaking point and wanted to escape by whatever means necessary. I was still active in church and trying desperately to continue my relationship with God, so I knew I couldn't take matters into my own hands. I felt bound.

As always, school was my refuge. Whenever there was some sports event, I would make it a point to attend, if only to stay away from home for a couple of hours. After a football game one Friday night, Jamie, an old classmate of my brother's who graduated the year before, asked me out on a date. I agreed to go out with him, but first I had to get my parents to comply. After my parents met him, my dad agreed to let me go on a date with Jamie.

Jamie and I dated and became an official couple shortly thereafter. We were pretty much inseparable. My parents liked him and allowed me to come and go as I pleased, as long as I was home at a decent hour. We continued our relationship throughout the rest of my high school career, attending my junior and senior proms, mul-

Better Than I Should Be

tiple football games, and my softball games.

Around Jamie everything was simple. He was always more concerned with what I wanted instead of his own needs. The only thing I wanted was to stay away from home as much as possible. Jamie was the kind of guy most girls would love to have: kind, caring, and sensitive. Selfishness was not in his nature, especially where I was concerned. He would change plans at the drop of a hat if I asked him. He had been that way since we met two years before.

Jamie was a constant for me: constant friend, constant giver, constant escape, constant recipient of my ill-placed resentment. He did not deserve the way I treated him most of the time. *Having someone that good should not have happened to me,* I thought. *No one could be that affectionate and love me without wanting something in return.* The world, my world, didn't work that way. Everything had a price, but which of us was going to pay that price? Only time would tell.

Jamie was faithful as always, coming to my rescue without the slightest idea of what I faced. There were very few days that we weren't together. For that moment, it was a win-win situation. My parents really liked him, so I could go anywhere with him, and he got to spend as much time with me as he could possibly stand. On the surface all looked well to him. But if he really knew the truth, what would he have done? He was not a fighter, so would he leave me stranded, too? When would I find someone to guard me and protect me?

Because of my warped perception of a healthy relationship, Jamie had unknowingly taken the brunt of my displaced aggression. Any other guy would have walked away. Yet he stayed with me. Constant criticism did not deter him. Sex had become a control issue with me. This time the role was reversed. I was not the one being controlled, but the one IN control. It was on my terms. Sex was also my biggest area of mental conflict.

After so many years of abuse, I had gotten to the point where I thought that no matter what I did, I'd never be pure in the eyes of God. That had been taken away from me. So why bother trying to be something I wasn't? Dreaming of one day getting married to the man of my dreams and my husband being my first was never going to be an option for me, as it was stripped away before I even had the chance to imagine it.

Here was where the conflict grew. I knew who God was and the difference between right and wrong, faithfully attending church while living a secret life. So, a war raged inside my mind that I constantly battled. I tried to do what's right, but consistently fell short.

Being that I was in control of my sexual encounters with Jamie, I could be abstinent for several months and feel like I was finally getting on track with God. However, at home, I was still being molested and raped (assault by penetration) several times a week. Changing my sad reality was unforeseeable, but I wanted to do what I knew was right by changing the things I could control. Jamie was probably so confused by my flighty mood swings. One minute I was telling him "no" and the next I was telling him "yes."

What did it matter anyway?! *God was not going to forgive me for letting someone violate me,* I always thought.

Since it was happening to me against my will, I might as well do it. At least I had a choice with Jamie.

As we get older, usually we have at least one relationship we wished we could have done differently. Honestly, I would have to say my relationship with my high school sweetheart, as many people used to call him, would be the one. I'm not saying we would have married, but I definitely would have treated him better. He was, and still is, a great person. The way I treated him was uncalled for and I regret it. He was the kind of guy who would have walked through fire to make me happy. Most girls would love that, right? Well, not me. I used it to my advantage. Don't misunderstand; I really did care about him. Our relationship was not always one-sided.

Looking back with a different perspective, I can see how controlling and manipulative I was. Our relationship was the one thing I felt I had control over. At home, I had absolutely no control over what was happening to me. By using his feelings for me against him, I could dictate where we went and what we did. If he didn't comply with my suggestions (sometimes demands), I would get angry with him. This usually resulted in him being too willing to do what I wanted the next time.

This again would make me angry, because I saw him as weak and indecisive. The poor guy couldn't catch a break with me. It's not that he did anything wrong; it's that I was dealing with the sexual abuse and rape/assault, and he had no idea. I guess I was waiting for my knight in shining armor to confront my dad and then take me away from all that hell. I blamed him for not being that man.

Eventually, this led to the ruin of our relationship. Since that time, I have wanted to apologize many times about the way I treated him. He didn't deserve any of it, no matter what my reasoning was. But on a positive note, our relationship was not always dysfunctional. We had our good times.

Throughout the majority of our relationship, I continued to go to church faithfully, although not everything I did reflected such. I still struggled daily with my home life. My faith in God was more evident during different periods within those years. I would strive to refrain from doing things that I knew didn't please God. It was during those times of staying close to Him that God gave me the strength to endure the abuse I was experiencing. Then there were the months when I would fall back into my depression and prayed Jesus would pull me out of this horrible situation I called life. Many times, I prayed Jesus would let me die, just to ease the mental suffering.

And here it is…BUT GOD! But God had a different plan, a plan that I could not see or may not have comprehended even had I known. Sometimes unanswered prayers are the best!

GLIMPSE OF HOPE

Not much for wearing dresses, I put on a pair of khakis and a multi-colored button up shirt. As far as dressing up, this was about as good as it got. Sunday was my favorite day of the week. I loved being around positive people and the chance to learn more about God. Questioning God had been a part of who I was for the last three-plus years, since my offender's return home when I was sixteen, but it didn't negate the fact that I loved God and possessed a measure of faith unknown to even me. My heart longed for the things of God, but my mind was tormented by the realization and imagery of my suffering. A particular Sunday in early 1993, however, brought with it someone who would be instrumental in changing my life.

Like every Sunday, I went to church alone. The greeters met me at the door and welcomed me just as they did every week. They asked how I was doing and I lied and told them everything was good, knowing that I couldn't say how I really felt. But I thought for the moment it was true. Entering the sanctuary, I said hello to most of the people. The congregation was small enough that I knew everyone. I felt somewhat awkward because I didn't fit in with any age group. I was nineteen and a college student. Finding someone my age who could relate was difficult. I was in this awkward period of transitioning from a teenager into womanhood. I still participated with the youth, but I also participated with the women's group. As usual, I just wanted somewhere to fit in.

That was when the pastor introduced him, our new music minister, Chap. The pastor reminded us of a visit by Chap and his college drama team. I remembered Chap very well, a cute dirty blonde with the most beautiful eyes I had ever seen. During that visit, a friend from school and I were so captivated by his eyes we were talking about him the remainder of the night. This wasn't the same guy. It couldn't be. His hair was darker. And his eyes...his eyes didn't have the same effect on me as before. Needless to say, I was very disappointed. Little did I know Chap would become a pivotal part of my life. After the service, I introduced myself and went on with life as usual.

Every once in a while, my brother Tom would let me use his truck to run errands. Living in the country, it was all about having a pickup truck. The higher it was and harder to climb into, the better. Tom had recently downsized to a smaller truck, but I still had to jump up into it

GLIMPSE OF HOPE

to get in. It was a small Mazda with large mudding tires. When I drove it or my dad's truck I must have looked like the biggest country girl redneck in town. I was not the girly-girl type, except for the long curly brown hair, and most of my wardrobe consisted of jeans, t-shirts, and the occasional long sleeve button up. Makeup had rarely touched my face, and I was thankful not to be in desperate need of it either.

One afternoon, my brother allowed me to drive his truck into town. In true country style, I rolled down the window, lay my arm on the window frame, and hung my hand over the side. One of my stops found me at the gas station on the corner in the middle of town. It belonged to a couple who attended my church. I always enjoyed visiting with them and talking. The store was modestly stocked with engine oil, belts, and a few coolers containing a mix of sodas, juices, and ice cream. The smell of automotive grease permeated the air as a draft made its way from the two car garage bays.

After grabbing a soda and taking a seat, I had a nice conversation with Ms. Jenkins. I talked to her about church things and the like. She was a great source of encouragement for me, even in the middle of all the hell going on in my life.

Better Than I Should Be

As I was in my brother's truck getting ready to leave, Chap stopped by the store also. Over the last few months, I had gotten to know him and he seemed to be a nice guy, despite my disappointment a few months earlier during the announcement of his arrival. However, Chap and his good looks didn't seem to disappoint many of the older women in the church, and they didn't mind saying it either. They often commented on how cute he was, though most of them were old enough to be his mother. For some reason, I started to feel a strange connection to him. Yes, he was handsome, polite, and respectful. Who didn't like a guy who was musically talented? Although none of this stuff made me think of him in a way any teenage girl in her right mind would think of him. Besides, he was engaged, and he was not available even if I thought of him in that way. Chap was probably the only guy I felt comfortable around without feeling threatened or vulnerable. He seemed like a big brother to me. Most of the male relationships I had were conditional, but this one was not. He didn't expect anything from me other than growing in my relationship with God. God knew the one thing I needed then was a closer relationship with Him, and Chap was a great motivator.

When I saw Chap, I leaned out the truck window to speak. That was the first time I saw her, his fiancée. She

GLIMPSE OF HOPE

was tall and beautiful, with long wavy blonde hair, not really the kind of girl I pictured Chap with, but I saw why he was. Chap and I had a short conversation while his fiancée Kris stood by his side. I didn't know that day I was meeting my new best friend.

That day was the beginning of my journey to freedom, all by the divine appointment of her coming into my life. I bet she didn't know what she was getting into when she befriended me. Once we talked and got to know each other, I noticed my desire for her friendship was becoming something different. I found myself needing her friendship… desperately needing her friendship. I felt as if my whole existence rested on her acceptance of me.

When in the latter part of my teen years, I had no peers close to my own age in my church, except a young girl named Gail. She was several years younger than me. I couldn't tell her what was happening to me because she wouldn't understand, and she could not do anything about it anyway. Kris was a different story. She was slightly older and I knew she would help me. My dependency was like an addiction. As long as I was able to speak with her at least once a day, I was satisfied for the moment. If I couldn't reach her by phone, I would drop by her house just to have that contact I needed to calm my anxiety. All the while, I expected Kris to help me out of the hell I was in. I never spoke to her about it. How unfair was that to put such high expectations on someone to do something they had no clue was happening? Little did I know she was doing exactly what I needed her to do...be an example.

In my mind, I had told Kris about my abuse hundreds of times. Too bad she wasn't a mind reader; but then again, it was probably better that she wasn't. There was one opportunity I had to tell her, and when I began my story, I couldn't bear to tell her the whole truth. What would she think about me? Would she quit being my friend? I wouldn't risk it. I needed her friendship too much.

I remember that day I missed my chance like it was yesterday. After multiple offers to accompany Kris back to her hometown, which was two hours away, she granted my wish. This was it, my big chance to tell all. Maybe she'd take me away from my perverted prison. I thought that when I told her, she'd understand why I needed her. I just wanted someone's shoulder to cry on and to hear them say, "You're safe. I'll take care of you." But not just anyone. I needed it to be her. After playing the words over in my head multiple times, I just couldn't do it. I couldn't tell her. However, I did tell her what happened in my childhood and why my dad was sent to prison. Still, I did not explain what was happening then and had been ongoing since his release, three years before. I couldn't. Instead, I prayed that she would figure it out.

Reflection

God places people in your life to help you progress. They may be mentors, spiritual leaders, or people passing through. And thank God for the young couple he brought into my life when I was 19. It was during that time that I was really struggling to follow God and deal with the situation at home. On one hand, I was doing the whole church thing; on the other, I was begging God to get me out of my present situation. At times I didn't care how He did it. I am thankful that I never completely saw suicide as an option, though I'm not saying I didn't pray to die when I felt like there was never going to be a way out. While I was suffering, God was saying, "It's not for nothing." Even though I couldn't see the end, God knew the end before it began. God sent me what turned out to be my life savers, by way of our new youth pastor and his wife. Over the years, they would come to be the biggest influence of my life. First, I met Chap. He was our youth pastor/music minister. Talk about having your hands full; he was doing a two-person job, but we (the church) appreciated what he was doing. I was just happy to have someone remotely close to my age going to church. The fact that we both used the same hair gel made me approve of him that much more. It's funny how most of the women in church thought he was the cutest thing, whereas I just thought he was a really cool guy. Shortly after he had started at our church, he got married. To this day I still wish I had gone to the wedding.

Kris and I joke about how we became friends. The first time we saw each other Chap failed to mention to her who I was, other than by name. She stood beside him while he and I carried on a short conversation. She occasionally joined in.

It wasn't until we were at church the next Sunday that we officially introduced ourselves. Kris jokes that she introduced herself to me so she could see who the competition was. At that point in my life, you can best believe I was the least of her worries. However, she needed to keep her eyes on some of those elderly ladies at the church, because they were a way bigger threat than me. But it was all in fun. I kind of took toward Kris, because she was the only female close to my age, except for one other friend who was a few years younger. She was a great influence to me when it came to living a true Christian life. I would spend as much time as possible with her and Chap because I was in a different atmosphere when I was around them. I didn't have to deal with the abuse or really even think about it when I was with them. I felt safe around them, even though they didn't have a clue what I was going through.

One day Kris asked if I wanted to accompany her to Virginia. She had some personal business she needed to attend to. While she was attending to her affairs, I stayed the day at her parent's house. She has great God-fearing parents and I felt comfortable around them also, which really meant a lot to me. As a matter of fact, I was so comfortable I took a nap on her parents' couch and I believe it was one of the best naps I've ever had. I still remember the dream I had during that nap! It was amazing how different I felt when I was around them, Christians who really love the Lord versus the evil that was going on in my home. It really was like night and day.

Having what some call an accountability partner is a great way to keep yourself from making a lot of stupid mistakes or wrong decisions. Not that I didn't make a lot of mistakes, but I based a lot of my right decisions on how or what Kris would think if she found out what I did. When I did make those mistakes, I could always count on her to tell me exactly why I was wrong. She was never one to break it to me easily. Instead, she would give me the harsh truth. Believe me, she wasn't much on giving me the sweet and nice version of anything. I'm sure that's why I respected her so much. What I didn't know about walking the Christian life, I could always see when I looked at her. No, she and Chap weren't, and still aren't, perfect, but I knew they had something in their lives that I wanted, a closer relationship with God. Over the next few years, under their leadership I became closer to God. I was baptized and also led a lot of my friends to Christ. There's no better feeling, other than getting saved yourself, than leading someone to Christ.

BACK TO REALITY

Over the next few months, I went through the motions as I always had. Nothing had changed at home. When my mom went to sleep, he came into my room. Immediately upon the door opening, I tucked the covers under me as tight as possible, hoping he didn't find his way beneath them. Again, I was wrong. The touch of his hand on my skin sent silent screams through my mind. As he found his way to places he shouldn't have been, I gritted my teeth and tears streamed across my face and down to my ears. Think of the shrillest agonizing scream imaginable. That was the scream locked inside of me, just demanding a way out. Imagine the most chest pounding, anxiety-filled heartbeat ever felt. That was the sound ringing in my ears. Imagine the grasp of holding on for dear life. That was the grip I held onto my pillow, covering my face. I was so mentally exhausted. When I awakened it was to the sound of the alarm clock.

As always, Jamie and I spent most of our free time together. I was still going to church religiously, trying to fit God into my bigger picture. So, doing the things Jamie and I did didn't come without conviction. However, the conviction was not enough to change the helplessness I felt, so I did it anyway. For Jamie, he thought having sex was fine because he intended for me to be his wife. I was doing it simply because I could. I was my own person and I didn't have to answer to anyone. Especially my parents.

The phrase "Daddy's little girl" had no positive connotation to me. To me, the thought was rather repulsive. Not that I didn't think it was a good thing for other father-daughter relationships, just not mine. What I wouldn't have given to have a normal relationship with my dad. What I wouldn't have given for a normal relationship with ANYONE! The relationship I had with my mom was strained because I felt she never protected me. How could she not know what he did to me? Or did she know and just not care? Maybe she too was afraid to face the truth. No matter what, someone was going to get hurt. Someone was already hurting.

How could I stop it? What were my options?

Tell someone? I couldn't face that again. My family already treated me like an outcast for speaking against him the first time.

Run away? I had nowhere to go that would offer any refuge.

BACK TO REALITY

Get married? I was young, but I was not dumb. Getting married would not solve my dilemma. It would only hurt Jamie in the end. How could I completely love someone if I couldn't even love myself? I knew enough to know I was not ready to be married.

Suicide? Hmmm...now there was an option...but not right now.

Keeping a busy schedule didn't seem to halt the detestable action taken against me. My father always found a way to fulfill his sickening desires. It was indescribable the frustration and anger I felt. No matter how much I begged and pleaded for God to fix it, He never answered me.

I was still there and so was my dad. Just the thought of his touch made my skin crawl and my stomach turn. He didn't see when I cried and clenched my fists in complete and extreme fury while he pretended I was someone I was not.

What purpose could there be for that? I tried to do what the Lord said was right, so why was I still in that situation?!

******

"Hey, do you wanna go with me?" The question came more as a command than a legitimate question. Immediately, I felt my blood pressure rise as anxiety crept its way into every nerve in my body, stinging my brain with thoughts of the reasoning behind his question. Nothing good could be behind his demanding invitation.

If I refused, he'd get angry.

If I went, I'd appease him, but betray myself.

Up to this point, what I felt and thought didn't seem relevant. With utter disappointment in myself, I gave my reply.

Living in a rural area allowed for ample opportunity for secrets. So many places to go where no one could see...or so you'd think!

The dark hung like a dirty shroud, giving the illusion of concealment, but thin enough to see through. The summer heat was still present, though the sun had hidden its light. Stretching a great distance, the dirt path seemed endless. I wasn't sure where it would lead me, but I knew the destination was not where I wanted to be.

I moved closer to the door of the truck in hopes of creating an impassable rift between us. Disappointingly, I was only an arm's length away. His hand inched toward me to find mine, as to affectionately make a connection. The only connection I felt was my mind's bitter resentment against him. Could he not read the expression on my face or was I just numb to the whole disgusting truth? The next twenty minutes or so were spent pretending this wasn't happening again.

Feeling dirty, useless, and shameful, I adjusted my appearance to reflect a façade of innocence. The mental visions of what happened made me want to be non-existent, but how? Those thoughts were brought to a screeching halt.

Two small sparks of light moved slowly in our direction. Growing ever closer, it was obvious a vehicle was making its way toward us. Undoubtedly, fear began to shake every bone in my body. Who was it? Would it finally be over, or should I say, "Just the beginning?" In my mind, I knew the person driving toward us would be Jerry. The path was part of his family's farm, and we were trespassing. What would he say?

The lights were closer now.

"Get down on the floor!" my father commanded.

There was no time to think. I did what I was told.

A male voice, not belonging to my offender, echoed

Better Than I Should Be

into the cab of the truck. It was Jerry.

"Hey man, you don't need to be out here. I don't care what you're doing or who you're with, but you need to leave."

"Okay, I'm leaving."

"And don't come back on this property."

"I won't," Dad said in agreement.

My heart felt as if it would race out of my chest, as the sound of the electric window separated the conversation. Cramps found their way through my legs as I sat in the fetal position trying to keep my identity from being exposed.

"You can get up. He's gone."

Unwinding my twisted body, I crawled back into my seat, as far away from him as possible. No matter how far I tried to inconspicuously move from him, he always had me within his reach.

The look on his face showed relief from what could have meant a life of imprisonment for him. For me, it would have meant freedom. So why was I equally as relieved?! I should have been screaming at the top of my lungs, "Come back! Help me!" but his very presence choked the words out of my throat. We slowly left the farm land and made our way back home.

Reflection

From the outside, I seemed to be doing fine, while the whole time I was still battling a seemingly inescapable situation. My life was one huge game of tug-of-war. I was caught between doing what God wanted and required of me and living a lie. When the bondage of an abusive relationship gets that immense, you begin to pretend it doesn't exist. I'm not saying you forget, but you try to live two separate lives. One life seems to be all smiles, like the world couldn't be better. The other is spent living in terror of when, not if, it will happen again. I wanted so badly to tell someone so I could finally be free. But I couldn't. I was threatened with the fact that if I did, my little sister (fifteen years my junior) would have to suffer the same perils of poverty that my brother and I did in our childhood.

The thoughts of how my mom struggled to provide for us was still fresh in my mind. I didn't want my mom or my sister to go through that again. So, I made up my mind that it was better for me to sacrifice myself so that

Better Than I Should Be

my sister could have the things I never did. This also meant that my mom didn't have to do things on her own anymore. As for my brother, I didn't really take his feelings into account, because he didn't have to suffer as I did. He could come and go as he pleased, never having to endure the abuse. I, on the other hand, had to endure the inconceivable.

My father tried to control me as much as possible without seeming too suspicious. It was not because I was a rebellious person, hanging with all sorts of shady characters. On the contrary, I would surround myself with positive people. They were my only means of maintaining my sanity. The control was the result of a power trip to show me who really called the shots. No matter what I did, I could never be free of his authority.

I TRIED, NOW I'M DONE

After high school graduation, I attended the local community college to participate in the Medical Assisting (MA) program. It was not my first choice. I wanted to attend the Physical Therapy program. I was placed on the waiting list for Physical Therapy, as this was a highly sought after program. With limited new student openings, only a few people were selected. The college had awarded me a full one-year scholarship at the end of my senior year in high school. Not wanting to let it go to waste, I chose the next best option, the MA program.

I had a full-time schedule, attending classes Monday through Friday from 8:00 a.m. to 3 or 3:30 p.m. While I was in college, my parents did not require me to work. Due to our family only having one vehicle, I still had to pick up my dad from work in the afternoons. During the fall months, I would have to wait for him late into the evening. My dad worked on a farm. The fall meant long harvest days. This did not leave much time in my schedule for a job. The only deviation from this routine was when I could have someone meet me at the farm and leave the vehicle for my dad.

When the town league's softball season rolled around

the following summer, I volunteered to be an assistant coach. I absolutely loved teaching the young girls the ropes and watching them develop their skills. I felt a sense of worth I rarely felt otherwise. I wanted to be a positive influence for these young girls and to encourage them. I also made friends with some of the parents and coaches. Those friendships spilled over into everyday life, not just at the ballpark. I invited many of them to church and for years we all attended together. Many hours were spent laughing, listening to music, and talking about everything from trivial things, personal issues, our latest favorite music, to how great God had been in our lives.

Many of my new friends became *chosen* family. I spent a lot of my time not only being friends with some of the girls (who became like little sisters to me) and their parent(s), but also was a sitter for some of those same girls when needed. This allowed me to limit the time I spent at home and averted any potential abuse, because I would frequently stay the night with my friends on the weekends.

As a result of Jamie always being at the ballpark with me, he came to know many of the people I now considered close friends. Jamie also accompanied me to my friends' homes countless times. This was mostly due to

I Tried, Now I'm Done

the fact Jamie was my ride for much of that time. Sometimes he would drop me off, and other times he would stick around. He lived a few miles away from some of the families, which was convenient for him when it was time for him to go home. Sometimes this was an irritation to me, especially when he would linger around and want to be with me. I wanted some space. Space that didn't include any kind of intimate physical touch or pouting because he wasn't the center of my attention. I just wanted to take time out of my chaotic life and enjoy some much-needed fun and laughter without thinking about anything but the present moment.

After the first year of helping coach the 7-to-12-year-old girls softball team, the next year I decided to not only coach them again, but also co-coach the 13-to-15-year-old girls' team. Unlike the younger girls, this team had to travel to local towns for games, as the immediate area did not have enough players for multiple teams. On Friday nights I would play with the church league. My days and evenings were filled with softball games.

Some of the older girls I coached would often be around the ball field on their days off because they had a sibling or two on one of the younger teams, or because they knew their friends would be there. With all of this time interacting with some of my older players and getting to know them, I became a sounding board and confidant to them. Taking on those roles would turn out to be more challenging than I could have anticipated.

I had my own troubles at home, so I wasn't ready when one of my girls disclosed she was being abused by her stepdad. My immediate reaction was anger, followed by a sense of needing to help create a safe environment for her when she was in my presence. This confession also brought with it some skepticism. As a result of my own abuse and my family denying the truth, I had this mindset that if you claim to have been abused in some way, you better not be lying about it. Proposing allegations of abuse when they are not true is disgraceful. Notably to those of us who endured abuse. A bad light is shown on victims the more people falsely accuse.

Needless to say, I didn't know how to handle the situation. I couldn't prove anything and even if I could, she would not admit it to anyone. Her stepdad was a wealthy and prominent individual in our county. From my understanding, many more illegal activities were centered around the home. She feared the repercussions and for her safety.

Who am I to encourage her to do something I cannot

I Tried, Now I'm Done

even do myself? I concluded.

One afternoon Jamie and I stopped by to check on her. We sat in the driveway talking. After some time, her mother came out and walked towards us. It was obvious she had been drinking. Instantly her mom started questioning us, wanting to know why we were hanging out so much. Obviously, I couldn't tell her it was because her husband was molesting and beating her daughter. Where was the proof other than her daughter's word? I was sure the girl would not have corroborated it if I offered up the allegation to her mother.

Instead, I was accused of wanting to have a same-sex relationship with her daughter. I adamantly refuted that idea. I had absolutely no desire to have that type of relationship. I guess I should have seen that coming at some point since her daughter carried herself in a masculine way and I, myself, wasn't a very girly girl. That alone may have given false implication. My main focus was to make sure her daughter had someone on her side, despite what she wore and how she looked. With this insinuation, I decided it was time for Jamie and me to leave.

After all the drama, Jamie and I returned to my house. Up until this point Jamie hadn't said much. But once at the house, he decided to give his opinion about my spending time with this teenage girl. Not knowing the reason and simply for the fact I didn't want his two cents on something he didn't know and couldn't understand if he did, I became irritated with anything he said. The weight of my own sufferings compiled with trepidation from external sources created a situation where it was just a matter of time before I hit my limit. I decided it was time for Jamie and me to go our separate ways.

Reflection

You would think participating in your favorite activity and being a part of something bigger than yourself would be a highlight in your life. In some ways, yes, it was. I look back on those summers coaching and playing softball with great fondness. Life-long friendships were forged during those years. Those were great and memorable times. But outside of those times, other moments brought with them disarray. One can only take so much misery and disappointment. Between the home situation, the clueless boyfriend, and stepping away from someone in need of a safe person to confide in who could also relate, my brain was on overload. I was overwhelmed; and I had to relieve the anxiety and pressure or I was going to lose it.

I Tried, Now I'm Done

There are those situations in life when you just have to accept your losses and walk away. Whether it be friendships, mentorships, or romantic relationships, it is not wise to remain in relationships that cause more harm than good. We, as people, were never meant to save the world, nor were we built to carry it. My mental load was lightened after I ended those two relationships. No longer did I have to brush off unwanted advances, nor did I have to feel responsible for helping someone with something over which I had no control. However, my biggest foe still remained at home.

After I was newly single, my days were somewhat routine. By this time, I had a modest position working for a radiologist at the county hospital. My job afforded me the ability to purchase my own vehicle. Having my own transportation not only made life easier, it also significantly reduced the occurrences of abuse I was regularly experiencing.

Church was very much still at the forefront of my life. I began to assist with the youth group I had been a part of a couple of years before. Things were not great, but they were looking up. Little did I know, four short months after my relationship with Jamie ended, my world would be turned upside down by one little question leading to a whirlwind romance then quickly ending in heartbreak.

1995 - PART I

At the turn of the new year and shortly after my breakup with Jamie, I wondered what this new-found freedom would bring me. In just over a month, I would turn 21, and I was still living under my parents' roof, still working full-time, and going to church every chance I got. Considering I no longer had to agonize over disappointing God with my pre-marital sexual exploits with Jamie, I felt hopeful my life would get on track with God. For so long I struggled mentally with all the shame and guilt I felt over my life. Could this be the time I would get the boldness to take control of my life?

For a few months, Jamie tried his best to win me back. I can admit he made a valiant effort, but I couldn't go back to the way things were. So when my birthday rolled around on February 3, after asking several times, I agreed to let him take me to dinner for my birthday. I told him up front that this was not a reunion, only two friends having dinner.

Jamie arrived at my house with a dozen of my favorite flowers, yellow roses. After placing the flowers on the kitchen bar, we headed out to dinner at Applebee's. The drive was somewhat awkward. The conversation

Better Than I Should Be

was unnatural. I didn't want to say anything to give him false hope, and it was obvious he wasn't sure what to say either. However, once we got to the restaurant, the night went without a hitch. We talked and had a nice time. When we received our food, he proceeded to ask the question many newly twenty-one-year- olds are asked when celebrating the milestone birthday.

"Do you want to order a drink?" he asked, expecting to already know the answer.

"Nah, I think I'm good," I replied.

Looking puzzled he comes back, "It's your twenty-first birthday. You don't want a drink?"

Again, I declined, "No, I'm good."

Even though this seemed odd to him, I couldn't care less about drinking alcohol. I tried it a few times when he and I dated and it only made me sleepy. I didn't see the hype of it all. Regardless, I was trying to be true to my faith. Drinking alcohol was taught to be unacceptable. There were also alcoholics in my family. I did not want to tempt fate.

Once the night was over, I thanked him for dinner and expressed that I had a good time. To avoid any more awkward moments, I gave him a hug, said my goodbyes,

1995 - Part I

and walked into the house. This was the final occasion I spent with Jamie.

A few days later, an older gentleman at my church, Mr. Doug, asked if I would be interested in going with his son to the Sweetheart Banquet for the church if his son were to ask me. I agreed to his proposal. The banquet was in less than two weeks, which meant things were changing fast and a chain of events was set into motion.

Because I agreed to Mr. Doug's proposal, sometime during that week I was to expect a visit from John, Mr. Doug's son. I knew of John from a former schoolmate of mine who had a major crush on him, but I had never met him. He was a few years older and had gone to a different high school. It was exciting to think I was possibly going out on a date with someone new after having been in a long-term relationship. This was all new territory for me.

My wait was short-lived. One afternoon after John was off from work, he drove the half-mile from his house to mine. I met him outside and he asked if I wanted to ride into town and go to the store for a drink or something. I immediately accepted and told him I had to let my mom know I was leaving.

I went inside and told my mom I was riding to the store with John. Never having seen John before, and

Better Than I Should Be

because she had not gotten over my break-up with Jamie, she was slightly unsettled with me moving on. She really cared for Jamie like a son.

"Who is that?" my mom asked suspiciously.

"That's John, Mr. Doug's son. You know Mr. Doug.

He goes to my church," I replied.

"I've never seen him before. I don't think you should be going with him. You don't know him," she retorted.

"He's Mr. Doug's son. They live about two minutes down the road from us. I'll be right back."

With that said, I went out the door, jumped in the car, and off we went.

On our little adventure, we carried on conversation as if we had known each other all of our lives. We talked about the obvious things: getting to know each other, work, mutual people we knew, shared interests; but he did not mention the real reason he had come to meet with me. Probably due to both of us talking so much, the topic had not made its way into the conversation. Before I knew it, we were heading back toward my house.

Pulling into the driveway, I was a little sad that we had to cut our encounter short. At no point did I feel un-

1995 - Part I

easy or scared around him. I genuinely enjoyed those first few moments officially meeting John in person and not only hearing about him from his dad.

Once he parked to drop me off, John asked me if I would go to the church's banquet with him. My heart may have skipped a beat from excitement, but I kept my composure and agreed to go to the banquet with him. We said goodbye and that we would be seeing each other soon. The date was set.

The first step was going on a mission for a dress. Yes, a dress. The banquet was right around the corner. Whatever I was going to buy needed to be done quickly. The local Belk department store was my first and last stop. After a short while of sifting through all kinds of dresses, I found it! The perfect dress that fit who I was personality-wise, as well as fitting nicely with my body type. Navy blue, very modest, mid-calf, with short sleeves, and two ribbons that tied in the back.

After the dress was selected, the shoes were next. My shoes were basic black low-heel pumps. These were harder to find than the dress because of my shoe size, a whopping 10.5 wide. This usually swayed me to pick the following size up. Walking in high heels *and* wearing a dress would have been a little much for me. My anxiety level was already peaking. Adding another anxiety-in-ducing activity, such as my discomfort in wearing high heels, would have distracted me from enjoying my date. I definitely did not want that!

In the afternoon before the banquet, I got ready at Chap and Kris's place. Kris had asked to do my hair and make-up when I first announced I would be going to the banquet, and I was happy to oblige her request. Had I done it myself, there is no telling what I would have looked like. I was not a big make-up person and she knew it. She decided to curl my hair in big, flowy waves as opposed to leaving my tight Mariah Carey type curls, and she applied just the right amount of make-up to my liking. Despite my nervousness, I was eager to see what the night held.

Once John and I were at the restaurant, we sat near his parents, Mr. Doug and Ms. Phyllis. The conversation between all of us was fun, with lots of laughs, especially toward me. I was so fearful of getting food on my dress, I used way more napkins than nearly everyone at the table combined. Mr. Doug and John thought it was amusing. I was slightly embarrassed, but not as embarrassed as I would have been had I stained my dress. I just rolled with the jokes and laughed with them. I didn't get offended or shy away. I actually liked the snarky remarks and the playful contention. I saw it as a challenge and I was very competitive, in a nice way. The night went wonderfully. Good food, good company, and a new possibility... perfect.

The following weeks were exhilarating. Almost every evening after work, John and I used his dad's truck and we drove the back country roads. He talked about his love of the outdoors, hunting and fishing, riding the four-wheeler, and wanting to build a car for track racing. There was a three-eighths mile oval asphalt track in our hometown, and it was the newest hotspot in the county. I talked about my appreciation for some of those same things, such as growing up in a neighborhood full of guys in the country, which meant a lot of four-wheeler and dirt bike riding. I also enjoyed fishing with my grandparents down by the Roanoke River and praying to God I didn't see a snake. As for the race track, that was new to me.

While we rode around deer spotlighting one night near the Voice of America broadcasting station, we came to a stop at a crossroads. We sat there for a minute or two, then John turned to me and asked, "Can I hold your hand?"

I quickly replied with a yes. My heart started beating in a rush. He thought, in asking, he would merely be holding my hand. But little did he know, at that moment, he would also be holding my heart.

It may not have been love at first sight, but it was awfully close. Approximately a month after our first date, my feelings got the better of me and I gave in to temptation. I wanted every part of John. I wanted his company, his time, his sarcasm, his jokes, his smile. The list goes on and on. This was the first time I had ever felt overwhelmingly enamored with someone. The thought of wanting to give my entire self to someone whole-heartedly, as opposed to being taken from, had never been something I ever really contemplated. The physical part was only a reflection of how completely close I wanted to be to John, with all of my heart and all of my soul.

After one more intimate encounter with John, I finally came back to reality and knew I had to get a grip on myself. I knew this wasn't how God created relationships to go. How could I disappoint God again by not controlling my fleshly desires? If I wanted our relationship to have the best possible chance, I knew we had to put a stop to what we were doing.

Therefore, I offered up a proposition.

Since the banquet, John had started going to church

with his dad. I remember John going to the altar and giving his heart to the Lord, and feeling thankful God had touched his heart. He knelt on the first step of the altar with the tip of his cowboy boots touching the floor. The boots stuck out in my mind because rarely had I seen him wearing cowboy boots. Knowing he had done this, I thought my proposition would be a good idea for both of us to get these urges and feelings out of our systems and see where our relationship went. The proposition was this: ONE LAST TIME.

To my delight and relief, John agreed. One more time and no more until we were married, if we decided that was the direction we wanted to pursue. He said he would work out the details on when and where. The hotel was booked a few days later.

This last hoorah was supposed to take some of the pressure off. Quite the opposite! It would become a monumental point in time for our relationship. Our lives were about to change forever. But for the time being, everything went according to plan. We were sticking to our guns…no sexual activity.

At church one late afternoon, John and I sat on the tailgate of his dad's truck talking when his dad walked up to us and joined the conversation. We discussed marriage

Better Than I Should Be

and children, and I blatantly stated I did not want any children. I had my reason, unbeknownst to anyone else. Mr. Doug's countenance dropped and with an almost weepy voice he said he wanted a grandson to carry on the family name. That grandson would have to be from John. I said we would worry about that later, but at the moment that was how I felt. All the while, I had no idea I was already pregnant with his grandson.

It did not take long to realize something was up. At first, I thought I had caught a stomach flu. Once I noticed I had not had my period, I started to panic. My proposition from a month or so earlier was now revealing its true consequence. Third time's a charm! To confirm my suspicion, I told John and we went to the store to get a pregnancy test.

He seemed to be cool with the idea of a baby. I worried what people would think of me: my parents, my family, my church family, and especially Kris.

We stopped by the college and we went inside to find a restroom for me to do the test. I wanted to know immediately. John waited right outside the restroom door to receive the result. I proceeded to take the test and sat it on the rear of the toilet. After throwing away the package and washing my hands, I walked back into the stall. I saw it instantly. A pink + mark became visible. My heart dropped. This was going to change everything. I walked out of the restroom and I guess John read my face.

"You don't have to tell me. It was positive, wasn't it?" He asked for confirmation for what he had already deciphered.

"Take me to Kris's house," was my only reply.

We walked to the car and John did as I asked. The car ride was mostly silent for the fifteen to twenty minutes it took to reach Kris and Chap's apartment. My mind raced a million miles a minute. Silent tears rolled down my face. A couple of weeks before, I had expressed that I did not want children. Now here I was pregnant *and* unmarried. I don't know why I thought God was going to be mad at me for getting pregnant.

It didn't catch Him by surprise.

We pulled into the drive and John asked if I was going to go in. I told him to give me a minute. As he exited the car, I asked him to ask Kris to come out to the car. He closed the car door and proceeded to go inside. I didn't want to walk in because I was embarrassed to say anything in front of Chap. I sat in the car crying while John was inside. Kris finally came out about five minutes later.

Better Than I Should Be

She opened the driver's side door and hopped inside and shut the door. She told me John had already told her about the pregnancy. I couldn't do anything but cry. She questioned me about John's and my relationship and what our plans were. She also said John seemed to be excited about the pregnancy. I told her we had discussed marriage recently and we would probably get married.

Her comment to that idea was, "Just because you're pregnant, you don't have to marry him."

Marrying him wasn't my issue. It was all about the timing.

We sat in the car for a few more minutes. Not once did she try to console me or show me any empathy. I could tell she was disappointed in me. So was I.

Then she said, "Come on in. Chap already knows." We got out of the car and headed inside. It was time to face the music.

John was first to tell his parents. I, on the other hand, was trying to be coy whenever I was around my mom and skated around the fact I was super nauseated. I was not ready to tell her my secret. Time was not my friend and soon the proverbial cat would be out of the bag. I did, however, tell my dad before I told my mother. It was

1995 - Part I

almost like a challenge I set before him. Not that I ever worried about the baby being his, as the rape I endured was considered, by legal terms, as assault by penetration. If he responded with anger toward John or me and made a big deal about it, I would also make known his secret. Although the abuse had slowed to a halt prior to dating John; the fact remained that he was guilty. He didn't want people to know what he had done, and I didn't want to hear his mouth about John and me. This situation was mine to handle. Not having my baby was never an option, nor was walking away from John. As far as I was concerned, John and I were in this thing together.

My mother never mentioned her suspicion of me being pregnant, though we both knew that she knew. I finally confirmed her suspicion and also broke the news to her that John and I were planning to get married. This was not exactly how I thought the conversation of me getting married would play out. On the other hand, when has anything in my life ever been done by the book? Why would this have been any different?

The wedding was set for May 12, only three months from our first date. I never, in a million years, would have speculated we would be getting married so quickly after the conversation in the church parking lot. Not only was

Mr. Doug getting the grandson he spoke of wanting, he was also gaining a daughter-in-law. I would rather have gotten married first and then pregnant. As God would have it, that was not the order. Babies are never a mistake and the untimeliness of this pregnancy was brought on by my own selfish desires to have one last fling before committing to abstinence before marriage. For someone who never wanted children, I didn't do anything to prevent it either. No one was to blame but me. On the other hand, I was about to marry the love of my life and our baby was a result of that love—admittedly, mixed with some carnal desire.

As the wedding date grew closer, many of the church women were excited and helped plan the reception and executed the events of the day. They rallied around and showed me great support and showed much love. These women had seen me grow up in the church from a small child into this young woman who was anticipating marrying her true love. Having had the ladies' backing was a great relief for my soul and for the shame I had been feeling.

John and I wanted Chap to be the minister to perform the marriage ceremony. However, Chap was not ordained at the time and could not do it. We decided to go with the

1995 - Part I

senior pastor. Subsequently, John asked Chap if he would be interested in being the best man. They discussed it and decided the best man for the job was none other than John's dad, Mr. Doug himself. By all means, he was the reason John and I met. Chap and Kris found their roles in singing a couple of choice songs during the ceremony. Kris also assumed the position of matron of honor. Everything started to come together.

At home, the tension was rather thick between my parents and me. My mom was Team Jamie and my dad didn't like anything about the fact I was getting married. Honestly, I was ready to leave and have my own life. Yes, I was scared. I also remembered the main reason I hadn't left to begin with, my little sister. Believing I could save her by staying was never going to work. It would only postpone the inevitable. I had to focus on what was in front of me: John and the upcoming birth of our baby. Getting married due to the pregnancy was not an obligation. My feelings for him were undeniable and I was ready to commit to forever.

Since my father did not approve of my upcoming nuptials, I had to find an alternative to take his place walking me down the aisle. The other prominent male figure in my life was my brother. I asked if he would do the honor and if he agreed, instead of wearing a suit or tux, I asked if he wouldn't mind wearing his dress Army greens. It didn't take a lot of begging or convincing. Just a little explaining about the dad situation. He accepted the task and affirmed to wear his dress greens. I appreciated his willingness to step in. One more piece to the puzzle was completed.

Decorations were purchased, the groom's suit was to be borrowed from one of the other men from church, and the wedding dress was rented from a local shop. Now that everything was in place, the only thing left was to say "I do."

On May 12, 1995, I married my friend, my partner, my confidante, my companion, my heart's desire. As I walked the aisle with my brother, looking sharp in his Army suit, I took in everything. The people who attended to show us support. The decorations. Ms. Martha Knox, who played the piano keys so beautifully. But most importantly, I couldn't wait to be beside the man standing in front of the candelabra waiting to take my hand and give me his last name. The ceremony was very quaint and humble. Traditional in most ways. I couldn't think of a better pair of people to be beside John and me. He had his dad and I had my best friend, Kris. He and I had each other. The moment was perfect.

1995 - Part I

As we stood together and recited our vows, I couldn't take my eyes off of him. Chap and Kris sang a duet during the early part of the ceremony, followed by Chap singing "Keeper of the Stars." When it came time for John to kiss his bride, I was a little embarrassed to be kissing in front of church folk. I leaned into his kiss briefly and pulled back quickly. There was some laughter throughout the crowd of guests. I blushed and smiled bashfully. The pastor then presented us to the people... Mr. and Mrs. John Johnson.

1995 - PART II

Settling into our new roles as husband and wife was fun and exciting. Getting to know each other came easy. We fell right into line. During those long evening drives when we were first dating, we learned we both enjoyed a lot of the same things: four-wheeling, outdoor activities, long drives with no agenda, and having conversations. We were almost inseparable outside of our respective employment.

Like all newlyweds, we had to learn each other on a more physical level. Obviously, John and I had gotten to know a little about each other, as we were expecting a child in the fall. But this was on a different level from anything I had experienced before. We had a home together and our own privacy. No more searching for places to be alone with each other. No more worrying about getting caught or worrying about who knew. At this point, it was expected.

The intimacy didn't come without some difficulty at times. For the most part, we had a healthy sexual relationship. However, my past abuse would rear its ugly head on occasion and was a matter of affliction and shame. It didn't matter how safe I felt with him, how much I want-

Better Than I Should Be

ed to be intimate with him, or how much I loved him, I couldn't disconnect my mind, will, and emotions from my body. One particular instance was so distressing it ended with a major hole in the closet wall.

John was always a gentleman when it came to sex. He never once made me feel I was obligated to be intimate with him. He didn't force me to do anything I wasn't willing to do. Be that as it may, there was this one instance in which I became overwhelmed and anxious while we were being intimate. John noticed I was sobbing with my hands over my face and he immediately attended to me, asking what was wrong. I couldn't answer him and just cried. He asked if it was related to what he had heard [about my dad] and I confirmed his suspicion. He got up out of the bed and walked into the closet and closed the door. The next thing I heard was a wail and his fist breaking through the closet wall. After he released his rage, he came out of the closet and walked over to me and crawled back into the bed and held me. My past was not only hurting me, but now it was hurting him, too. I apologized profusely. I never meant for my damage to hurt anyone else, especially him. We did not have a lengthy conversation. He didn't interrogate me. We didn't walk away from each other trying to avoid the topic. There was an understanding that something awful had happened to me,

1995 - Part I

and this was our quandary to face. However, this was only one area of struggle that would wreak havoc on our marriage.

Only a month or so after our wedding, John's struggle with crack cocaine resurfaced. Prior to our marriage, I knew little about John's past drug abuse. I was aware he had spent a year in jail due to charges indirectly related to his drug use, but not much more than that. However, he did have one instance of relapse within the first month of us dating. Never having used any type of illegal substance, I was very ignorant to the world of drugs. How they could consume and wreck your life. How they control your thoughts and entice you to do things you wouldn't dare do if not for the cravings. How they can cause physical illness. How they drive you to push away the people who care about you. The list could go on and on.

In a very short period, we experienced a lifetime of heartache due to John's drug use. He would stay out until all hours of the night. I learned from his dad what John's MO was when he was using. Thankfully, John's parents were our neighbors and I had them close for support. I wanted to find a way to help him through this.

Because I feared for our future and our unborn son's future, I tagged along whenever he wanted to leave the house. I wanted to counter any chance of him straying off and going to purchase drugs. Even this was an issue, as I didn't want to feel as if I had to babysit a grown man. I was sure he didn't want to feel like he needed one either.

At first, John was very dispirited over his condition, to the point that he begged me to stay home from work one day to be with him so that he wouldn't go out and buy drugs. My main concern was for my husband. I made the call to let my manager know I wouldn't be coming to work that day. As we lay there in bed, I held him and reassured him I was not going anywhere. I was going to be right there beside him.

I'm not sure how they found out, but Chap and Kris came over that morning to check on John. He and Chap talked in the living room, while Kris and I talked in the bedroom. I explained to her what had transpired that morning and why I had not gone to work. I was at a loss on how else I could help John, other than physically be with him every minute of the day. That would prove to be unsustainable. No amount of love could make that possible, no matter how hard I tried.

Our marriage soon became an absurd roller-coaster with an overabundance of twists, turns, ups, and downs. It would have caused mental whiplash if there was such a

1995 - Part I

thing.

There would be stretches of times where life was great, like the times we spent out on the river. Sometimes it was just us, and other times we would go fishing and checking perch pots with Mr. Doug. During the good times, we also went four-wheeling or go-cart racing. It was nice being together and not having his drug problem looming over our heads every second. For a period of time, John attended NA (Narcotics Anonymous) meetings each week. I know he was present because I accompanied him. The meeting leader and attendees agreed I could come in so I didn't have to wait in the truck. When things were good, they were good. When they were bad, they were really bad.

In the times when John would relapse, I spent hours driving all over the county searching for him. It didn't matter the time of day or night, I would take my scared, angry, very pregnant self and get in my vehicle and drive. I was never scared for my safety. I was scared I would find him dead from an overdose or that he would reject my attempts to appeal for his return home with me. Many nights I was unsuccessful in my search. The few times I did find him, usually driving around, I would stop at the nearest place we could park. I begged, cried, and pleaded

Better Than I Should Be

for him to just come home.

In November, we welcomed our baby boy into the world. After being induced early that morning, I had not progressed in the birthing process as quickly as they were expecting. I was taken to the operating room for an emergency c-section around one the next morning. I was placed under general anesthesia and it would prove to affectme emotionally once I recovered and was able to stay awake. I had no desire to hold my son. I was extremely lethargic and melancholic. We had several visitors come in to join us in welcoming our son. Kris was one of those people. She held our baby before I did. She offered him to me so I could hold him, but I declined. It would take some time before I felt comfortable holding him and caring for him the way a mother should.

Because of this, John and his parents really stepped up and took the reins in helping take care of our boy. Not only was I dealing with postpartum depression, I was also dealing with post-surgical recovery. Mentally and physically, I was not doing well. I did slowly start coming around and spending more time taking care of our son. The more responsibility I had in taking care of our baby, the more I felt uneasy about some of the physical care I was expected to do. Diaper changes and bathing were

1995 - Part I

the two tasks that caused the most distress for me. It felt shameful to touch my son while cleaning his bottom. I would rather John take care of those duties. My feelings were not because I was lazy, but because of my own internal controversy. I never shared the reason for my reluctance with John. Unfortunately for me, my reluctance was behind many of the arguments we had regarding our son. I didn't want to feel that way and I wasn't sure how to fix it. Nonetheless, I was a mother and I had to assume every aspect of the role, despite how I felt. How life can change, all within a year!

I would like to say things were better after our family grew by one, but it was more of the same. Good times, followed by bad times, followed by good, then followed by total ruin. The drug use was still an intermittent hardship, and I, in turn, became the nagging wife. We eventually headed in different directions. He was dealing with his drug use and eventually chose infidelity. I was clingy and always hounding him about things I disapproved of. Before I knew it, I was asked for a separation period, from which we never recovered. My heart was torn.

Better Than I Should Be

Reflection

Love is an unpredictable force of nature. If you are blessed enough to ever experience true love, you'll never forget it. The way your heart races at the sound of the person's voice or the anticipation of seeing him or her, if only for a moment. Not to mention the utter disappointment when plans of seeing them do not work out. The feeling in your chest is undeniable; it's like you cannot breathe and an elephant is standing on your chest. It is hard to focus your thoughts on anything other than being with this person. Although, it is different from infatuation. Love is a beautiful, chaotic mess of true emotions. To say I was not ready for what was about to happen is an understatement, especially so soon after splitting from my long-time high school sweetheart.

Only four brief months after I called off my relationship with Jamie, I found myself presented with a new proposition. The way it happened was a little unconventional, but interesting nonetheless. An older gentleman from my church approached me one Sunday with an unusual request. The question went something like this, "If my son asks you to the Sweetheart Banquet, will you go with him?" I thought, why not? It is just one dinner date. Besides, if it gets awkward, I will be there with my friends and I can just join in on their conversation. So, I agreed to go. What harm could it do?

One thing I have learned in my many years on this earth is...NEVER ask that question! I'm not a big believer in Murphy's Law, but there are instances when I have had my moments of suspicion. I like to look at the positive side of things. I cannot say that has always been the case, though. I'm grateful that I have changed over the years. I have overcome too much not to be optimistic. God brought me through unimaginable situations and I would hate to dishonor Him by thinking negatively about everything. However, this new chapter in my life would be the beginning of a new set of challenges, challenges for which I was very ill-prepared.

My Valentine's date led to one of the most beautiful and exciting, yet shortest, relationships of my life. I never imagined I could feel that strongly for any single human being. Boy, was I wrong. Immediately I fell into this vast black hole called love. I say black hole because it just sucked me in and I had no sense of my surroundings. There was only one thing I could see and that was him. Our relationship evolved so quickly, I barely had time to breathe. I got pregnant within the first couple of months and that was not how my life was supposed to go down. Did I regret it?

Absolutely not. However, the timing could have been better.

Maybe I should have focused more on that breathing!

Within months, my life took a 180-degree turn. I was no longer a young single woman with unlimited possibilities, but a young wife and mother. Learning to be a wife was hard enough. Adding a child to the equation created much more to the stresses of being a new bride. I knew absolutely nothing about either. My not-so-distant past also did not help the situation. The childhood abuse always found a way to affect everything I did, from my sexual relationship with my husband to having reservations regarding caring for my new baby's physical needs. Bathing and diaper changes were my least favorite because I did not want to be accused of inappropriately touching my son. This also caused arguments between me and my husband because I could not tell him I felt uncomfortable taking care of our child.

Our marriage began its downward spiral rather quickly. Despite all of the love I had for my husband, it was his recurring drug use that led to our demise. No, I was

1995 - Part I

not the perfect wife and I own up to my part of our failed marriage. However, drug use was the main catalyst of our split. With his addiction consuming our lives, we never had a chance. A love like that may fade, but it never completely goes away. At least it did not for me. There were fond moments of remembrance, but it was usually followed by relief of not having to experience the bad times ever again. Well, maybe not with him, which leads me to my next challenge…

SECOND TIME AROUND

I got my life back on track with God. Everything seemed to be going great, until I got some really upsetting news. Kris was the one person I knew I could always count on (regardless of the fact she always called me a thorn in her side), but she moved and left me on my own. Looking back at my track record, I knew making my own decisions led me to terrible outcomes. I had come to depend on this friend's wisdom and her relationship with God. I figured God would give her the answer before He would give it to me, because I had messed up so many times. Ordinarily, I counted on her to tell me what I should do when I had challenging decisions to make. And as you might know, God was getting ready to give me a rude awakening.

Once I was single again, I moved right back where I didn't want to be, with my parents. Over the years I found that was where I always returned, facing those same demons all over again. Yet during the two years between my first and second marriages, I found myself back where I should have stayed all along, in the church. It's there I found comfort, peace, and belonging. My friends Chap and Kris once again helped me regroup during a short period before they moved away.

I did it again. I made a decision that would consume the next eight years of my life and prove who I was and what I was made of. That's when Kenneth came back into the picture. At this point, I was in my mid-20s, a single parent with a decent job, and a faithful follower of Jesus Christ. I didn't have any immediate worries other than a strong desire to move out of my parents' home. I admit it was convenient at the time to stay there, but all of that was about to change.

One day out of the blue, I got word that Kenneth was back in the area. A mutual friend with whom I attended church asked if Kenneth could have my number. I agreed. After several phone conversations over the course of a couple of weeks, we decided to meet at his sister's house where he was staying.

My initial reaction to Kenneth's return was excitement, because he was my first teenage love. This was my chance to find out what might have been. Remembering what an amazing guitarist Kenneth was when we were teenagers, I cultivated this grand idea of him going to Virginia to play his guitar with Chap and his worship team. I traveled to Virginia to visit Chap and Kris at their new church every chance I got. If I could convince Kenneth to

SECOND TIME AROUND

consider it, I could finally leave Martin County and move to Virginia. With all of my wishful thinking, I failed to see how controlling Kenneth was.

Not long after our reunion, I became pregnant with our daughter, thus forging a permanent connection with him. We were married within a month's time of learning about my pregnancy, after a substantial amount of pleading on his part.

Something was telling me not to get married, but did I listen?

No. I guess some things really do have to be learned the hard way.

The first couple of months of our marriage were pretty good. Marriage took some adjusting on both our parts, but we made it work. Wedded bliss didn't take long to change, though. My past was getting ready to haunt me in a big way. Only a few short months after our marriage, Kenneth began using drugs. I was devastated, since I had gone through the same situation in my previous marriage. While we were dating, I asked Kenneth if he had ever done hard drugs. He emphatically denied ever using anything more than marijuana. My response to him was I would not date anyone who had done hard drugs because of the things I went through in my first marriage. Again, he assured me he hadn't.

Boy, was I wrong for believing that one!

During this relationship, I vowed to myself that I would stay in church, because I knew it was my only hope. Despite my willingness to go to church each week, it didn't always work out as I had planned. Kenneth was so controlling I had to sneak out to go almost anywhere. Even when I let him know I had to go to the grocery store, Kenneth would not allow me to leave. Instead, he would go by himself. I had become a prisoner in my own home.

Kenneth was aware of my past and my dad's incarceration. Once we became married, he constantly interrogated me for details about the sexual abuse. Based on his behavior, I felt it was not wise to give in to his requests for such details. However, I did confirm that the abuse resumed shortly after my dad was released from prison. A downward spiral in our marriage began at that point.

The pursuit of knowing my past led Kenneth to some exceedingly dark places in his mind. These dark thoughts often caused severe arguments between us. According to Kenneth, the thought of my abuse is what led him back to hard drugs. Yes...back.

SECOND TIME AROUND

Until that first night he didn't come home, a couple of months after we were wed, I believed he had not done anything other than marijuana. I was worried something horrible had happened to him. I called all the area hospitals and everyone he might be with. All the while I had this gut feeling, so I was praying I wasn't about to go through another marriage with an addict.

Kenneth showed up at my place of employment around 2 the next afternoon. I noticed him as he pulled into the parking space directly in front of the office entrance found at the end of the building. My work office was located at the far left end of a mobile trailer, which was shared with the insurance and billing office staff for the local hospital. The building sat in the back corner of the hospital's property. Because we did not get much traffic in our section of the parking lot, I was always quick to notice when someone pulled up. In this case, I was hoping and expecting all day for Kenneth to arrive at any time. When he did show up, I was thankful I was one of only two people working out of this billing office. My manager was the only other person to see Kenneth arrive.

Already anxious from not knowing the where and why Kenneth didn't come home, I hurriedly walked out to interrogate him.

"Where have you been?!" I asked in nervous anticipation of his answer.

"I was at my friend's house playing [guitar]. I told you that's where I was going. It was late and I had a few beers. I fell asleep," Kenneth responded.

"You couldn't call and let me know? I called every hospital I could think of to see if you had been in an accident or something." In that instant I felt my blood pressure rise as my face began to turn red.

Kenneth's rebuttal, "I'm sorry," was the only comeback he offered.

After trying for several minutes to get some real answers, I asked the question I thought I would never have to ask, "Have you been doing drugs?!"

The look on his face gave me my answer immediately. As he made general apologies, I felt my heart sink in my chest and rage throughout my body. I couldn't let it get to me.

I had to go back into the office and finish my day.

I concluded our conversation by telling Kenneth we could talk when I got home. I felt so defeated as I walked up the porch steps and back into my office.

SECOND TIME AROUND

The drug use became out of control. Kenneth sold things from our house, stayed gone for days, and stole to get a fix. Any money I had to my name, I had to hide so that he wouldn't take it. I hid money anywhere I thought Kenneth wouldn't find it or where he wouldn't look. This included everything from putting it inside my pillow to inside the hem of the curtains. Most of the time this didn't work. He became verbally abusive and threatening. To avoid further escalation, I would surrender to him what he wanted.

Things were so bad, I called my cousin Patty, who lived in Virginia, and made plans to leave without Kenneth knowing. In the process I had decided it would be better for my son to move in with his dad temporarily until I could establish work and my own place. This way my son would be in a stable location and not moving from place to place. John was sober at the time and doing good. It was the best option at the time.

Things didn't work out as I had planned; I stayed a total of two days with my cousin and realized I couldn't live there. Nothing to do with her, just that the living accommodations needed extensive work. I moved back home. Because of being back with Kenneth, John and I decided it would be better for our son to live with him

Better Than I Should Be

for the time being. Days, weeks, and months turned into years. Not until he was a teenager would he come back to live with me.

NOT AGAIN

"Wait 'til I get off of work! I'm coming to find you. Who do you think you are, taking all of my money, knowing it is the only income we have coming into the home?" These were the thoughts racing through my head as I waited for the clock to signal my exit.

How did I let this happen again? I had two children who depended on me. I couldn't keep living this way.

Something had to change.

Chasing Kenneth down was a regular occurrence. He always found a way to get my money before I could. Why did he do it? Simple, it was one way to fuel his drug habit.

On one particular day, I did not back down. I had a family to provide for. I went to find him and get my money back!

As I pulled into the familiar driveway of his drug buddy's home, I felt my chest pounding from the adrenaline-laced anger. That anger overshadowed any common sense I had. I should have worried about what he might possibly do in his drug-induced state of mind. At the moment, though, I didn't care. I was furious that he had once again failed our family, failed me, and that I let him do it. When would I learn he was not going to change?

I walked up onto the back porch of the old white house. After several knocks and some yelling at whoever might be inside, Steve opened his door reluctantly.

"Where is he?" I demanded.

"He's not here."

"I know he's here. Now tell him to come out."

It was not my intention to force my way in, but I pushed past Steve after several attempts to get the truth. I made my way through the kitchen to an adjoining room cluttered with stuff that would make even a hoarder anxious. I pushed through, trying not to fall onto the piles of trash, dirty clothing, and old furniture. All the while, I called for Kenneth to show his face.

After wading through the rubbish, I carefully found my footing to make my exit and on to the next room. Steve insisted that Kenneth was not here, but my instincts said differently. With every denial from Steve, I became angrier and more frustrated. I stormed through the guy's house demanding to speak to someone he declared was elsewhere. I was the trespasser. Steve could have had me arrested, or worse, he could have physically hurt me for

NOT AGAIN

entering his premises uninvited.

All that aside, I only had one agenda: find Kenneth and get my money back. This had happened so many times; Kenneth's well-being was not a concern to me. If he wanted to ruin his life, I did not care at that point. I had traveled that road too many times and it always ended the same—a few months of sobriety and then it was right back to using. I continued through the living room to the bedroom. This room was also cluttered, but cleaner (if that was what you want to call it) than the last. Upon entering the room and calling out for Kenneth, I noticed a mattress propped against the far wall. If I were hiding, that would be the ideal place. Without moving the mattress to expose what I assumed he was hiding behind, I placed one hand on the wall and another on the corner of the mattress and repeatedly kicked into the triangular space between the two.

Within seconds I heard pleading to stop my attack. The mattress was quickly pushed away and Kenneth was exposed. In his attempt to get away from my forceful strikes, Kenneth managed to push a hole into the drywall. That hole was the least of my concerns; I was on a mission. I was a mother fighting to provide for her children, even if that meant fighting Kenneth.

Better Than I Should Be

Once Kenneth got his bearings, he began his verbal assault. An argument ensued. I was usually a laid-back, easy-going person. But if you saw me there, you would not ever believe that. Kenneth knew how to bring out the worst in me. I spoke words I would never say outside of our altercations. Just saying them caused conviction and seemed so foreign to me. Knowing I am a Christian, Kenneth was quick to point out my transgressions as if to prove I was not as humble as I strived to be. He always knew how to make me feel bad about myself, especially when it came to my past. His attempts to make me feel shameful were his way to cut me to my very soul.

But I wasn't emotionally going there that day. He could say whatever he wanted; I did not care. I came with a purpose and I intended to collect.

ON SECOND THOUGHT

Once the drug addiction became life-consuming, I began to question everything. How did I let myself get into this mess again? Is the sanctity of marriage tolerant of such abuse and neglect? How could I change my situation? Rest assured, I considered everything I knew about my position as a Christian wife to find a reason I should stay and work things out. Looking back and remembering who God wanted me to be, I realized He didn't call me to be someone else's doormat. After seven years of total chaos, I was pressed to make a choice. Not just for me, but also for my children. My visitation with my son was hindered due to Kenneth's involvement with me and his drug use, while my daughter was being uprooted several times a year whenever we had to move on to the next place. I made the choice that turned out to be one of the sanest decisions I had made throughout my entire second marriage.

In 2005, my season changed. Due to all the abuse I was experiencing, I sought a Domestic Violence Protective Order (DVPO). The local Department of Social Services' Victim Advocate listened to my dilemma and explained the process to me. After my initial visit, I was hesitant to go through with filing to get the DVPO. I was afraid of how it would work logistically and with guardianship of our daughter. Kenneth never hurt or abused her in any way directly, so the DVPO was only regarding my protection. I knew if he was able to visit with our daughter, he could easily take off with her in retaliation and to torment me further. Neither of us had sole legal custody, which would allow this to be easily done. I was not ready to take that chance.

Months went by and conditions did not change. It was a constant whirlwind of turmoil. Then it happened. Kenneth spoke words that would make my decision obvious. While we were lying in bed one morning during one of our "on-again" phases, he told me he had thought about killing me. Prior to that moment, I had never heard those words come out of his mouth. That's when the lightbulb came on! I finally realized I could be in imminent danger under the right circumstances.

After hearing those words, I again found myself speaking with a DSS Victim Advocate. This time I made the choice to follow through with the DVPO. Once Kenneth was served the papers, it was the beginning of the end. Things seemed to get quiet during this time. Even in the quiet, I always waited for the ball to drop. It wasn't

ON SECOND THOUGHT

a matter of "if" he would contact me. It was a matter of "when." The DVPO was only a paper and offered no physical protection in the event he should decide to violate the order. It offered little comfort in how I felt about my safety.

One night when I was home alone around midnight, he showed up. I had not heard from him for a few months thanks to the stipulations of the DVPO. I guess he reached the point he no longer cared about the order or he hoped I would not turn him in. Kenneth parked his car near the rear of the house, where it couldn't be easily seen from the road. As I stood in the kitchen, which was opened to the main living space at the rear of the house, I heard him as he exited his car and proceeded to make his way across the deck to the back door.

My home, one of the many we once shared, had a large deck on the backside, which was one of my favorite features of the house. At first, the knocks on the wooden door were soft. With every unanswered attempt, they grew more intense and accompanied pleas to open the door. I waited, for what felt like an eternity, for him to leave. My movement inside the house was minimal, because I didn't want him to know I was awake and aware he was there. He was determined to make contact. At that time, I didn't own a working cell phone, nor did I have a traditional landline, so calling for help wasn't possible.

After a long stretch of time, I finally decided to engage in conversation with him. I did not open the door, however. My sofa was perfectly situated adjacent to the window beside the back door. I raised the blind, but never opened the window. I then took a seat on the arm of the sofa facing the window. I asked why he was there and what he wanted. Petitions for me to let him in so we could talk lasted another thirty to forty-five minutes. My reply was, "Say what you need to say. I need to go to bed because I have to work in the morning."

After approximately two hours of back and forth through the window about wanting to talk and now needing gas money (you can insert your own headshake here), I guess he finally had enough.

He threatened, "If you don't open the door, I'm going to kick it in."

In my most exhaustive yet unreserved tone I said, "Then do it!"

The next thing I knew, my back door flew open and I ran toward it and out onto the deck and into the yard. To my surprise, Kenneth had startled himself when the door

ON SECOND THOUGHT

had actually broken open and fled into the yard in the opposite direction. At that point, I was extremely ticked off.

We argued as I got in my car and tried to leave. Before I could close my door, Kenneth ran over and placed one hand on the door jamb casing, while placing the other hand on the top interior portion of the driver's door. He held the door open, hindering me from escaping.

That's when I remembered something: Kenneth had once bought a wooden stick tool known as a "Tire Buddy" while he was working with a transportation company. This stick was a sixteen-inch by one-inch round dowel with two inches of metal wrapped around one end. Tire Buddies are typically used by truck drivers to do quick tire pressure checks by hitting the tire with the metal end and checking the rebound of the stick off of the tire. The further the stick rebounded, the more air the tire had. If it did not rebound far from the tire, then the tire usually needed more air. Good thing I remembered I kept it in my car for protection, in case I ever needed it. If ever there was a time...

I reached underneath my seat and pulled out the Tire Buddy. Several times I demanded Kenneth to step back and let me leave. He resisted one too many times and I swung the Tire Buddy to the best of my ability, considering how I was blocked in my car. The blow landed on the upper side of his forearm that was holding open the door, hitting directly on top of the bones. Kenneth immediately retracted his arm and yelled he was going to call the police, also while screaming,

"You broke my arm!"

I begged him to call them. I knew what the outcome would be. I made it clear that it would not be me who would be arrested, because he was the one breaking the DVPO.

Evidently his arm was not broken, but bruised, as shown by his quick regression to former discourse. By this time, it was well after 3 a.m. I was tired of arguing and had resolved in my mind that if he wanted to hurt me, he would have done it hours ago. I regressed into the house and expressed to him I was done and going to bed. I'd like to say I was able to go directly to sleep, but relationships can be messy and emotionally complex. Not until after we had sex was I able to finally go to sleep.

The following morning, I got up and told him I didn't have any gas money for him and to leave before he was caught there. If any of my family came by, they would think I willfully let him stay. Plus, I was ready to leave for work and didn't want to be late. I already knew I had

ON SECOND THOUGHT

to report the incident. Whether or not he was caught at my house that morning, he was going to be arrested for breaking my door and violating the DVPO. When I arrived at work, I made the call.

Within forty-eight hours, I got word Kenneth had been arrested. Straightaway, I felt relieved. During the issuance of the DVPO months earlier, there was a contingency of a one-year sentence of mandatory jail time upon violation. With the knowledge of him being out of the picture for the next year, my anxiety eased. I had one year to get my affairs in order and dissolve that crazy marriage before someone got seriously hurt.

For the first time in a long time, things began to turn around. After Kenneth decided to kick in my door that night, I found myself moving to another home once again. In the course of our marriage, we had moved no less than ten times in eight years. Some of those moves were together and others were not. This was finally a new start for me. Most of my time was spent working, going back to college to finish up my degree, and with family.

The year 2006 brought with it some exciting events and achievements, as well as some not so exciting, but necessary, events. My first major event of 2006 was the purchase of my new-to-me vehicle, a red Dodge Duran-

Better Than I Should Be

go. While I was waiting for the paperwork, I walked over to the booth of a local pop radio station under a tent just beyond the showroom doors. A Spin-It-To-Win board was available for anyone willing to give it a try. I was feeling particularly happy, so I figured I would try my luck. And what do you know, I won a CD. Not just any pop CD, but an up-and-coming Christian pop artist, Stacie Orrico. New music to play in my new ride.

Shortly after I bought my Durango, several major events unfolded within the next six months. The first one began with a night of the worst chest and abdominal pain I had ever experienced. Nothing I did eased the pain, but I didn't want to wake my daughter to take her to my mom, nor did I feel like driving that far. Once the sun came up, I couldn't wait any longer. I had to go to the emergency room. I got my daughter settled in the vehicle and was planning to take her to my mother. That plan was cut short when I drove past the hospital. I took a left at the stoplight and made a beeline straight for the hospital's emergency room.

Once at the admissions desk, I used the receptionist's phone to call my mom to come get my daughter. My mom arrived with my grandmother approximately thirty minutes later. My night-owl grandmother didn't stay long

ON SECOND THOUGHT

because it was 6:30 in the morning. She was just there to drop my mother off, so that she could take care of my daughter and drive me home. From how it looked, I was going to be there for a while, so my mom decided to take my daughter home to our house to grab a few things. I gave her my keys to the Durango.

After a couple of hours, a GI cocktail, and an ultrasound, it was determined I was going to need surgery. I had a gallstone the size of a peanut inside me. I was thankful the reason for my pain was easily recognized. Upon discharge from the emergency room, I walked back to the admissions desk and asked to use the phone to call my mom.

As I was about to dial her number, one of the ER nurses came up to the desk and told me to put the phone down. I looked at her in confusion. I wasn't sure if they wanted to do the surgery right away or what. She told me to meet her at the triage room door eight feet over to my left. The nurse opened the door and proceeded to tell me not to be alarmed, but my daughter and mother had been in an accident and were in the emergency room.

Essentially, as I left the emergency room, my mom and daughter were being wheeled in by the mergency medical techs through the ambulance entrance. The

127

Better Than I Should Be

nurses had my mom and my daughter in two separate rooms. My little girl was sitting on a hospital bed with a small stuffed animal the EMTs gave her to help calm her. She had no injuries. However, my mom was strapped to a backboard in an adjacent room. Following some testing, my mom was released with just some bumps and bruises. What was supposed to be my mom coming to watch my daughter and driving us home turned out to be me finding all three of us a ride home. My Durango was now sitting at the dealership awaiting the insurance adjuster to decide if it was a total loss.

Two weeks later, I had my first of two surgeries that year. I had a cholecystectomy (gallbladder removal) in March, followed by a medically necessary breast reduction surgery in June to relieve severe shoulder and back pain. In the middle of all this, I was also able to finish my first college degree program and graduated with an associate degree in medical assisting. All of this was in the first six months of 2006.

The next six months were just as momentous as the preceding months. It was during this time that I sought legal counsel to pursue a divorce and legal custody of my daughter. It was time to put the abusive relationship behind me. Once the ball got rolling, it went quickly, with no hiccups along the way. Not only did I get the divorce, I also won full SOLE custody of our daughter. When asked if he wanted visitation, Kenneth expressed to the judge that he felt he didn't deserve it. The judge followed up promptly with letting Kenneth know he would have to petition the court to receive any visitation in the future.

Finally, the nightmare was over.

Reflection

I cannot count on my hands the number of times I found myself in situations similar to this one. Being this was my second marriage, I always felt I had to make it work no matter how difficult it may have gotten. I felt like a failure when my first marriage ended in divorce, so I was determined to make the second work. Kenneth, on the other hand, did everything possible to destroy the one thing we claimed desperately to want, a wonderful marriage. I will not make excuses for either of our behaviors, as we both made mistakes. His demons seemed to be more than both of us could handle. I do believe we could have made it if he would have taken his issues seriously and sought the help he so greatly needed. I was willing to work for my marriage, but I was not willing to live the rest of my life being controlled by someone who was verbally and emotionally abusive.

It is hard to believe that was the same guy I fell in love with so long ago at the age of fifteen. Sometimes teenage love should be left as that, teenage love. Wondering what might have been is oftentimes better to remain a mystery. But one thing I will never regret about the love we once shared is the amazing daughter we have.

One might think having two failed marriages, I would denounce the institution of marriage all together. If anything, these two divorces have given me a greater appreciation for those who have made their marriages work and who genuinely love and respect one another. I am not so naïve as to think any couple has had the perfect marriage. Disagreements, arguments, harsh words, slammed doors, walk-outs, often followed by long solitary walks or drives, happen. Relationships in which a husband and wife decide to unconditionally love, forgive one another, and understand marriage is not for selfish people are the kind I admire. Marriage is meant to be a selfless and willful exchange of sacrifice to and for each other. Anything less is negligent management of a relationship God has deemed holy. We all fall short. However, that's the beauty of grace. True love extends grace. True love understands

ON SECOND THOUGHT

we have our bad days, our sad days, our sick days, and our "I don't like you right now, but I still love you" days. True love recognizes the importance of sacrificing, because it places immeasurable value on what it considers to be irreplaceable and vital to its existence. The one thing we should all strive for, in any relationship, is true, genuine love for one another.

GIVE ME A BREAK

After having a crucial year of life-changing events, I hoped the new year would bring some much-needed relief. I looked forward to the future. With Kenneth out of the picture, life showed some improvement. Finally, I didn't have to worry about unwanted visits at all hours of the night. No more wondering where he was and if he was going to show up at my job unexpectedly. I had room to breathe.

My sister and I bought a mobile home together and located it on our parents' property in late 2006. It was a fixer-upper, but it was paid for. I spent my spare time doing repairs in early 2007. I laid carpet in my bedroom and in the living room. I also replaced the toilet and flooring in my bathroom. I placed off-white textured wallpaper on the top half of the bathroom walls and added wooden railing to separate it from the sand-colored painted paneling on the bottom. My sister had given birth in January and I needed to get the house ready as soon as possible.

My sister, her husband, their son, my daughter, and I moved into our new-to-us place once it was livable. There were two master suites, one at each end of the mobile home, which gave us much needed separation with plenty

133

of space. My intention was to live there long enough to pay my dad back for my half of the mobile home (as he paid for it up front) and to save enough money for a down payment on my own home. Since my sister and her husband would still need a place to live, I would forfeit any ownership of the mobile home. That was never meant to be my final destination.

A couple of months after moving in, I discovered some shocking news that shook my world. While at church one Sunday, an old middle school friend of mine revealed to the church that her daughter had been molested by a close relative. Having experienced the same, I went to her house that afternoon to talk with her. We sent my daughter, who was just shy of being eight years old, into one of her daughters' rooms to play while we discussed what had happened. I explained to her my history of being sexually abused and the impact it had on me. She did the right thing by facing the issue and not hiding it. It was going to be a long road ahead, but necessary.

Once we got home later that evening when my daughter and I were settling in for the night, she began to ask me questions about what she overheard at my friend's house. I was very careful in how I responded. It became very apparent I needed to be concerned with her line of questioning. Fearing the obvious, I asked the question I never wanted to ask.

"Why? Did something happen to you?"

The look on her face told me the answer.

"Did somebody touch you where they shouldn't?"

She shook her head no.

"Did someone show you something they shouldn't?"

That's when her head dropped. No physical touch had been initiated, but it was evident she understood something inappropriate happened.

Immediately rage seared through my body, but I couldn't let my daughter know. I didn't want her to think I was angry at her. I had been careful to restrict her from being alone with my dad.

I wanted to ask how it happened but I knew that didn't matter. What did matter was that I needed to do something about it.

I hugged my daughter and told her everything was going to be okay. I sincerely meant it.

Sometime after my girl had fallen asleep, I called Kris. She was still living in Virginia and not where I could talk to her face-to-face. From the sound of my voice over the phone, it was evident I was livid. Between my heart pounding and the resentment-fueled tears falling down my face, I felt like I was going to explode. I expressed to Kris how much I wanted to go and kill my dad for his actions toward my daughter. She calmed me down and suggested my daughter and I move to Virginia and stay with her and Chap for a while. With this invitation, I had an exit plan to take my daughter away from all of the craziness. There were only a couple of months left of school. Once she was let out for the summer, we would start the transition to Virginia.

In June of 2007, my daughter went to live with Kris and her family. I stayed back to continue working until I could find employment in Virginia. I took a day off from my job at home whenever I needed to attend a job interview in Virginia. Due to living out of state, I had difficulty finding employment. Between spending weekends with my daughter in Virginia, or Kris meeting me halfway with her so she could be with me for the weekend, the separation and lack of progress became frustrating. It had gotten to the point I was not content with anything: my job, my church, my living arrangements, nothing. I knew it was time for me to leave.

Give Me A Break

In the middle of July, I had one of those days where nothing unexpected or overly-dramatic happened, but I was irritated to no avail. It was that day I decided to hand in my resignation. As I was leaving for the day, I gave my manager, with whom I had great rapport, my resignation notice. I decided I would finish out the remainder of the month, which gave my employer a two and a half weeks' notice.

Now that a timeline for moving to Virginia was in place before securing employment, the pressure was really on. I had no savings and only two days of paid time off (PTO) left, which meant I needed to start working immediately after I moved to Virginia. Since I had such a hard time getting interviews during those couple of months, I didn't have much optimism I would get one so quickly.

On my last day, Wednesday, July 31, I said goodbye to my friends and coworkers. My PTO would cover Thursday and Friday, but after that I was at God's mercy. I wasted no time packing my SUV and making my journey to Virginia. There was a great deal of relief and anxiousness going through my mind simultaneously as it was an exciting new start, yet it was also rife with uncertainty.

During the two days I was officially on PTO, I

searched the Internet for every medical facility with an open position that I felt qualified to work. I spent no less than twelve hours a day sending resumes, filling out applications and making calls, while Kris and the children hung out by the pool. As much as I wanted to be outside with them, I knew my priority was to procure employment as quickly as possible. My diligence paid off.

One of the medical offices I sent my resume to responded late on Friday and wanted to interview me Monday morning. This was my first sign of hope, though I did not stop submitting resumes to other employers. The position would be forty-five minutes to an hour away in horrible Hampton Roads traffic Monday through Friday. No employer-based insurance or fringe benefits were offered with employment. However, time wasn't on my side and I would have to take the first reasonable offer.

Monday morning, I arrived for my interview. The office was a small psychiatrist's office. I had an encouraging time interviewing with the office manager and the office assistant. We had light-hearted conversation also and seemed to mesh well. Despite how I felt about the interview, I left with no expectations. They still had more people to interview that same day, and I had done interviews several times when I still lived in North Carolina

Give Me A Break

and I had had no success.

Within the next hour of returning back to Kris's house, I received a call. It was the office manager with whom I had just interviewed. She expressed how she and the office assistant really liked me and thought I would be a great fit in their office. She then offered me the position and asked when I would be able to start if I accepted.

My reply was, "What time do you open in the morning?!" She gave me the time and I told her I would be there first thing in the morning.

After a few celebratory declarations, I thanked God for working it out. I had tried for two months to get a job and it wasn't until I was living in Virginia that the job offer happened without delay. I only missed one day's pay. There was no other explanation for the rapidity of acquiring employment than God's provision. He did it, not me. Sometimes He requires us to make the first step. Moving to Virginia was that step.

My new living situation with Kris and her family was a temporary arrangement. The stress level of my circumstances didn't change after gaining employment. It only shifted from one concern to another. I ended up being offered a better paying position with benefits at the children's hospital located closer to where I was living. I worried about disappointing my current office manager as I enjoyed working with the ladies in the office. I had to do what was right for my family and that meant providing for them. I was responsible for my children's health insurance needs, as well as other financial obligations. Since my son was not living with me, these were legal obligations through my child support order. This new position would meet those requirements.

Things became even more interesting after my daughter and I ended up moving out of Kris and Chap's home with no plans of where to go next. I was grateful that another single mom offered to let us stay with her and her son. She was retiring from the military at the time and needed to find housing elsewhere. We decided we would find a home for rent that would benefit all of us. Around three months later, we found a nice two-story home a few blocks from the Chesapeake Bay. Our new place provided each of us with our own space to retreat.

With all of the new expenses, money was extremely tight. I subsequently had my SUV repossessed and was constrained to taking public transportation to work for the next year. Admittedly, I was frustrated with having to take the bus to and from work. However, the experience gave me some new perspective on how my life had and would

Give Me A Break

continue to change. I met some interesting characters and made a few acquaintances along the way. The long ride home from work in the afternoons allowed me ample time to begin writing my story. I valued the uninterrupted moments that allowed me to sit with my thoughts and put them on paper to one day share with others who need to know they're not alone.

Due to the lack of transportation, every other weekend I rented a vehicle to go pick up my son in North Carolina to bring him to stay with us. It was crucial I didn't let this setback interfere with our visitation time. Despite my struggles, I kept positive and was determined to make the best of this new life for me and my kids. They were my main focus, outside of my relationship with God, of course. My life was streamlined to my faith, my children, a few inner-circle friends, work, and obtaining my bachelor's degree. I wasn't interested in adding anyone new into the mix. I didn't want to divide my attention any more than it already was.

While on one of my trips to pick up my son, something happened that threatened my newfound solace. I was not expecting anything to catch me off guard, especially after I had worked so hard to keep my own notions of an intimate encounter with someone in the far reaches of my mind. I had been so concentrated on life in general, I didn't think about how long I had been without sex until my son's dad brought it up in conversation. I should have shut him down right then and there, but I was still drawn to him even after all that time.

INDISCRETION

What did I just do?! Okay, it was just a moment of weakness! Not to mention, I never got closure after John and I divorced. This just goes to show how a not-so-innocent conversation and some unresolved feelings can lead to something regrettable. I told myself, "This can never happen again." It would be easy to blame my past for my irresponsible decision, but I could not use that as an excuse. The truth was, an opportunity presented itself and I was not strong enough to resist it or maybe I didn't want to resist it. Maybe I needed to know exactly what my feelings were. Did I still love him or was I truly over our failed relationship and it was just a physical notion? Whatever the reason, it definitely revolved around him and not just for the sake of being with someone. Otherwise, this never would have happened.

The fact that I was in such mental disarray told me one thing: those unresolved feelings were no longer there. I was completely over him. It was not that I didn't remember what I once felt, but that it was now a thing of the past. Boy, did I feel horrible for allowing myself to give in! So much so that I wrote a poem to reflect exactly how it made me feel. I had to get those thoughts and feelings out. My emotional and mental health depended on it. "God, forgive me," I asked. Never again would I make that mistake.

Here is the poem I wrote:

Wipe it Clean

Remembrance of the past determines my choices

Fighting, but following the unholy voices

With all of my being I wish it were right

And could conquer the war of my internal fight.

These thoughts overtake, they consume my mind.

Lord, heal my heart like the sight for the blind,

Wipe the slate clean; release me from my past.

I can't take anymore; how much more shall it last?

Deliver me, Lord, from this once-holy bond

Until all remnants of "Us" have vanished and gone.

Ease the pain that my heart must endure.

Set my sights back onto the things that are pure.

INDISCRETION

I pray, dear Lord, that You've heard what I've spoken

'Cause I choose to follow You, though my heart has been broken.

Reflection

After I moved to Virginia, my daughter and I would make the drive to North Carolina to pick up my son from his dad's house. Life seemed to settle into a rhythm for me. Work, church, and college courses filled my days. Every other weekend I would have my son home with me. I never knew what to expect when I went to pick him up. Over the years there were periods where John and I got along great, usually during his periods of sobriety or if he and his wife were getting along that weekend. There were a few occasions I would leave promptly to avoid any confrontation.

As our son got older and his stepmother was no longer in the home, it was easier to communicate with John about our son. Some of the problems my son seemed to be dealing with regarding his stepmom, the person John had the affair with when we were married, were not an issue anymore. She did not treat my son the same as her children with John. According to my son and unbe-

Better Than I Should Be

knownst to me, she was abusive to him.

On one of my trips to drop my son off, my daughter and I stayed for a little while to hang out. This wasn't unusual, as we had done this many times over the ten or so years. This night was different, though.

Up until this point, neither ohn nor I were ever outside of a relationship at the same time. I had been married for several years to Kenneth and had divorced three years prior. John had been separated for several months with no plans to reconcile. This led to a conversation I never expected to have with John again in my lifetime. He and I always knew how to converse about anything. Talking felt natural with him, not forced. At first we had light-hearted, everyday conversation. The conversation slowly moved to our relationship status, such as how long we had been single, how long it had been since we last had sex. After we disclosed our answers to each other, it was John who made a proposal this time.

He suggested that we tell the kids we were heading out to the store to pick up a few things, but instead we would really take a detour and reset the clock. I was torn between doing the right thing and following my heart. I still loved him and never had true closure over our marriage. I chose the latter. When we returned back to the

INDISCRETION

house, we had nothing to show we had ever made it to the store.

In the moments after we were back, I had so many thoughts and emotions flooding my mind. I was glad I had the chance to tell him and express exactly how I felt about him. All the while I knew that would be the last time I could justify, in *my* mind, being with him in that way. I needed to know it was really over for me. That date has been solidified in my mind as the night the clock stopped...14 years and counting.

John asked if my daughter and I wanted to come over and spend more time by staying the weekend whenever we wanted. I acknowledged the offer, but I knew this was not the route I wanted for my life. I could not rationalize going from girlfriend, to wife, to ex-wife, and then to friends with benefits. The next time I planned to be intimate with someone would be with my future husband. If that never happened, I still decided my relationship with God and taking care of my children were my most important priorities.

WORK IT OUT

Before I could follow through with what God had planned for me, I first had to work on me. While writing this book, I came to a major standstill. My drive to finish was no longer there. My spiritual walk had become stagnant. When we are followers of Christ, we should have this overwhelming sense of desiring and being filled with the things of God (also referred to as living water).

In John 7:38, Jesus states, "He that believeth on me, as the scripture hath said, out of the belly shall flow rivers of living waters." Well, the water was there, but it wasn't flowing. It was not being stirred up. I had dammed it to the point it was slowly growing things that were killing me spiritually and also poisoning the purpose God had given me. Once I verbalized my struggle, I began to work on removing the dam so the water could begin to move again, so I could move again.

During a Tuesday night prayer meeting, I was asked for my prayer request. Most of the people were asking for prayer for physical healing, but I did not. I could have rattled off multiple physical needs. However, I knew I needed more than just physical healing. I desperately needed mental, emotional, and spiritual healing. The best way to describe my spiritual health was one word…numb. It was so easy to go through the motions, but the feelings of any kind of connection to God were absent. Having been a Christian for the majority of my life, I became very familiar with hiding my feelings [or in this case, the lack thereof] and presenting a façade of well-being. Deep down inside I knew I had to take a step toward total surrender. I would like to say I did on that night; however, that did not happen, though the process did begin.

As a result of the prayers that Tuesday night, I began a twenty-week program specializing in relational and sexual wholeness. My spiritual desert was about to have an oasis! I knew it would not be a cake walk going through this program. During the interview process prior to attending the program, it was made very clear the different emotional stages I would experience. I was thoroughly informed.

Being my stubborn, rebellious self, I attended the first several teachings with a "Why am I here?!" attitude. I knew I had forgiven all my past offenders and felt I did not need to revisit those places. What I didn't realize was I wasn't there to forgive, but to receive healing for myself.

The first spark of any kind of thought-provoking

came when I shared the story of my ever-evolving relationship with Kris. As I mentioned in an earlier chapter, I had placed my mentor and friend on a pedestal on which she didn't belong. Those ideals had long been discussed and resolved. Why should they be rehashed? My small group leader for the program suggested I pray to break emotional ties. I met this suggestion with some major defensiveness. What she was suggesting felt like betrayal to me. How could I break these ties without deserting my best friend? After several minutes of discussion, I decided to say the prayer, not for breaking emotional ties, but for breaking *unhealthy* emotional ties. I left the retreat that weekend feeling lost and disloyal. The great thing about this traitorous act was it became the catalyst that led me to process all the thoughts and feelings I had and would have throughout the remainder of the program.

Several days after allowing myself to process what had transpired at the retreat, I felt I needed to talk with Kris about what I had done and how it made me feel. Kris, being the friend she is, was very understanding and brought some much-needed encouragement. Although I understood what I experienced at the retreat was not directly about her, I did understand that it was necessary for me to go through that process to begin my journey to healing.

Better Than I Should Be

During the program, we discussed broken boundaries. I still had not fully committed to opening up at this point. After the corporate teaching that night and convening to our small groups, something changed. I stayed quiet until the other members of my group had a chance to share their stories, thoughts, and feelings. I tried to put my own thoughts in order; then it was my turn.

The best way to explain what was going on was a bunch of IEDs going off in my head all at once. I had so many memories and thoughts but no real emotional reaction to them, not until one of my group leaders opened up the door to something for which I was not prepared.

I began my sharing by speaking on how emotionally, mentally, and verbally abusive my second husband was to me and how boundaries were broken within our relationship, followed by the distance I felt with my son during his infancy. As a result of my childhood abuse, I felt like I couldn't change or bathe him for fear that someone would accuse me of being inappropriate with him. I shared how I was not only abused by my father, but several others in his absence.

That's when my group leader compassionately laid her hand on my arm and told me how she felt compelled to pray for me throughout the preceding week and had

WORK IT OUT

some verses she felt she was supposed to share with me. She read the verses carefully, engaging me in the moment. Following the scriptures, she began to share what God had laid on her heart. Those words were the exact ones God knew I needed to hear. What I had fought so hard to hold in finally came forth. I allowed myself to take in the healing words only God knew would open my mind and spirit to Him so I could move forward in my healing. It was made plain to me that night that what I had experienced as a child and into my teenage years was never God's intended plan for me.

Now that I was reminded of God's love for me, what next? I couldn't continue being and feeling like I had for the past year and a half. During our session it was said that God wanted to trade the armor I had been wearing (for way too long, I might add) for a garment of peace. I'm not even sure what that would look like. I'd been in a battle for my life for as long as I could remember. Was there ever a time I wasn't? The following day proved to be a mentally distracting one. I could not concentrate on my work. All my mind could think about was what had happened the night prior. In all of that beautiful chaos of thoughts, God revealed a new perspective to me. He began to give me understanding of two things: me now and me as what I affectionately refer to as "Little Tina."

Better Than I Should Be

My mind carried me to a vision of this young girl who suffered so much in her early years that ultimately led her to the place I am now. The whole concept was a little confusing at first, but the more God put the puzzle pieces together, the more it made perfect sense. That young girl was me, Little Tina. I felt so much compassion for her (Little Tina), not necessarily for me as who I am now. It was like we were/are two different people, but I knew we were also one. The more I envisioned Little Tina, the more protective I felt of her, like it was my responsibility to make up for all the mess she had experienced. I needed to make her present life the best it could be. That is exactly what I intended to do!

UNEXPECTED

Christmas Day 2014. It sure was unusually hot for December. I was dressed in jeans and a t-shirt with no jacket required. The weather didn't invoke that familiar Christmastime vibe that I'm used to. Walking toward the house, I saw that children were outside playing with their new toys, while other family members were gathered in the house or in small groups on the front porch. I did not make it home very often, so it was a little awkward when I first arrived. Once the "Look who's here!" declarations died down, I settled into my usual laid-back self. I was home.

Seeing family was nice. Visiting home was usually convenient because my aunt and uncle lived beside my parents. They shared the same driveway, large enough to occupy the two eighteen-wheelers my dad and uncle drove. My family was filled with truckers and mechanics. The women were generally homemakers or worked as seamstresses or housekeepers. Over at my aunt's house, I found most of the women gathered around the kitchen table, and the men hung around outside and tinkered with some automobile or mechanical device. I made my rounds, paying attention to not leave anyone out. I said my hellos and got the latest on what was happening in their lives, then I grabbed some food from their holiday feast.

My parents made the short two-hundred-foot journey next door to my aunt and uncle's place to show their sociability. My dad took caution to keep his distance and avoided being in close proximity to the children, as he was well aware of what could happen if he were to ever find himself in a compromising position. This usually meant we would gather outside in the open to carry on our conversations.

While hanging outside, my daughter and I passed out presents to my brother and his wife. I was super excited to give my brother his present. Tom had always been a pro-wrestling fan for as long as I could remember. As a teen, he would imitate his favorite wrestlers on a daily basis, saying the wrestler's most popular catch-phrase or striking their signature pose. Giving him a DVD of the Ultimate Warrior's most memorable matches was one the best gifts I could give him. When he opened the package, we began to joke about his on-going old-school wrestling obsession and his affinity for retro cartoons, like *He-Man*, and more currently, anime, especially *Dragon Ball Z*.

After a couple of hours, as I was about to announce

UNEXPECTED

our departure, my dad requested I take a walk with him so he could speak with me in private. I was curious to know what was so important we needed to go walking alone to have a conversation. I agreed to his request, and he grabbed my hand and led me toward the open road in front of my parents' house. I was nervous about what the conversation would consist of, and I wondered what everyone else was thinking, seeing us walking and talking outside of earshot.

"I wanted to let you know I've been seeing a therapist for a while and I've realized what I did to you was not right, and that it hurt you. I'm trying to work out my issues and the therapist said I needed to let *you* know that *I* know what I did was wrong. So…what do you think?"

"I'm really proud of you for going," I replied. At that point, I was completely baffled. This was not what I expected, not that I even knew what to expect, and on Christmas Day nonetheless! I wasn't sure how to respond to his acknowledgement and apology. "I'm glad you decided to go to therapy," I reiterated in my bewilderment.

We continued our awkward, but necessary, conversation until we found ourselves back in the yard with my sister and my mother. No one asked about what was said, and I was not about to talk about it and dredge up old wounds. I wanted to leave my family on a good note and them with the memory of a happy Christmas. We said our goodbyes and my daughter and I proceeded to my car for our two-hour journey back home to Virginia. My daughter hopped into the passenger's seat, as I sat dumbfounded in the driver's seat. As we began to drive, I explained my perplexed expression. "You'll never guess what just happened!"

"What?" my daughter inquired.

"Uh…my dad just apologized to me."

My daughter, being wise for her short 15 years of life, asked, "How does that make you feel?"

"I'm not sure. Mad?! I don't know!" I felt distressed. "Why 'mad?'"

"Well, when I decided I had forgiven him, it was MY decision. I did it because I wanted to forgive him, not because I had to forgive him. Now, I have to because he apologized."

The more I thought about what had taken place, the more annoyed I became. On one hand, I was trying to understand this was a great thing. He finally acknowledged his crimes and was getting help. On the other hand, I felt as if he had just violated me all over again. By apologizing, he took back control over something I had the control to do…forgive.

Reflection

This incident goes to show that even when you think you're in control, you're really not. God can flip the script on you at any time. I began questioning myself and God. Did I really forgive my father? Why was I so angry? I'd always thought I was owed an apology, so why was I angry when I got what I believed I deserved?

For a solid week, I wrestled with these thoughts and with the concept of not being in control of my own convictions and how I could live them out on my own terms. After deciding to forgive my father for sexually abusing me, I thought I would always have that over him. Forgiveness was mine and no one could take that from me.

But that's when I realized something. His apology was not meant to negate my forgiveness of him or to gain control. He needed to apologize—and really mean it—for him to heal. Once I accepted that he could no longer control me and that he, too, needed to apologize and heal as much as I needed to forgive and heal, then I experienced what true freedom in forgiveness felt like. The power of forgiveness is astonishing. It's now that I can walk in the undeniable fullness of forgiveness and live a more fulfilling life.

FORGIVENESS

Forgiveness is a word that creates massive amounts of emotional responses. One may feel a reaction of relief, while another may become aggressive or despondent. Some seek forgiveness or contemplate forgiving and others may be resistant to forgiving or accepting forgiveness. Whether you are in need of forgiveness or deserve an apology, forgiveness can be challenging. I learned this when my father apologized to me on that Christmas Day a few years ago. At first, it felt like he took my control away from me again. I had to realize only I had the power to control whether I should forgive or live in bitterness.

It doesn't seem like it should be that complicated, but for many it is one of the most arduous undertakings they will ever confront. When left unspoken, an apology does not retain the ability to create healing. It leaves room for bitterness to grow. You may have heard the saying, "Unforgiveness is like taking poison but expecting the other person to die." There is so much truth in that statement. Not only does unforgiveness cause mental and emotional pain, but it can cause physical ailments, too. If only we as a society would take time to understand how powerful and freeing the act of forgiveness is and apply it to our

Better Than I Should Be

lives, just think of how different the world would be! You may be thinking, that will never happen! People are too selfish and self-centered to ever let that be. Well, you may be right. There are a lot of narcissistic, self-absorbed people in the world. However, it does not mean we should not forgive or ask forgiveness. The only things you can control are your own actions and responses. So, whether you are in need of forgiveness or in the position to forgive, do it now. Ask that person to forgive you and do it sincerely. If you've been wronged, extend forgiveness. It does not matter if they acknowledge their wrong-doing; it would be nice, but it is not necessary. Odds are they may not even know they offended you, or they may have forgotten the incident altogether. We are usually the ones who hold on to the offenses. It's time to let it go. It is time to be free. It is time to forgive and ask forgiveness.

I do not speak of forgiveness or unforgiveness lightly or from a position of not having to do either. As I have stated earlier, I have had my fair share of offenses and of offending. There has been more than enough opportunity to allow bitterness to rule my life. Saying it that way may seem a little extreme, but that is exactly what bitterness does: it takes over. Negative thoughts start out small and then the more you allow those thoughts the quicker they turn into actions. Next thing you know your life is con-

FORGIVENESS

sumed with bitterness. Many times, we blame God for allowing someone to offend/hurt us, or if you were the offender, for the offended person not accepting your apology. One of my favorite musical artists quoted Timothy Keller saying it like this, "Worry is not believing God will get it right, and bitterness is believing God got it wrong." One thing I promise is He never gets it wrong. God is such a loving God that He allows us to make our own choices. The unfortunate part is we live in a fallen world and have to deal with the consequences of our decisions, as well as others' decisions. This permits substantial room to be violated and to become bitter. Being a bitter person is not an attractive characteristic, my friends. Don't allow it to take up residence in your mind, soul, or your spirit.

Remember this: God did NOT get it wrong and He says forgiveness is not optional. If we believe and follow His Word, we must forgive in order to be forgiven. Forgiveness has to be from the heart. Otherwise, did you truly forgive? By choosing forgiveness, you will be making one of the most liberating decisions of your life!

TIME VERSUS WOUNDS

How do you know when you are finally free from your past? It has been said, "Time heals all wounds." I believe that without facing the hurt, time only prolongs and masks it. Life comes at you fast, which makes it easy to get caught up in the *now*, suppressing and potentially snowballing the effects of your past and current wounds. The past does not go away, even though you feel you may have moved on. Until you deal with your past, it is always going to be there waiting for its chance to disrupt your life. The sooner you face your past, the sooner you can step into your future, the future God has for you. Do not deny yourself the life God has planned especially for you. That life does not come by simply living. It comes by taking control of every aspect and allowing God to be the center of it.

Too many times we try to find our comfort, even our identity, in the approval of other people. We need to make sure we do not allow people, that God sent to help us, to become a substitute for God Himself. Despite their intentions, people will disappoint you, often not knowing they are doing so. We should not put expectations on others for the things we should surrender to God. I have been guilty of this far too often. God is my source, not people. It is true He uses people to carry out His will, but we (I) should recognize the source of our help and appreciate and acknowledge those people He used to meet that need. Do not let a person become an idol in your life. Remember, God is your source in all things.

LOVE ME

One of the greatest challenges I faced after removing myself from the place of my past was learning who I am and how to love myself. I appreciate the fact that God made me a strong and independent person; however, I had not learned to love myself as an individual outside of being a mother, friend, or helper to those in need. Being alone always seemed to heighten my anxiety, which led me to seek shelter in the presence of those close to me. Those unresolved notions of falling prey to another predator were subconsciously etched in my brain. It never occurred to me that I had suppressed the real reason behind my apprehension of being alone. I really believed the reason was because I genuinely liked the company.

Enjoying personal quiet time or treating myself to a solo dinner was not who I was. Several of my friends told me how they made time alone for themselves. In my mind, all I could think was how boring and lonely that must be. In retrospect, I see I was the one who was lonely and always craving to be in the company of those who were content with their aloneness. In fact, they would make it a point to have their alone time. The benefit of that kind of time took years for me to understand.

Better Than I Should Be

It was not until recently that I finally decided to give it a try. My journey to self-discovery began with a simple, "Table for one." At first it felt a little awkward. The judgmental glares were more a figment of my imagination than actions of the unsuspecting diners who failed to notice my uneasiness. Thoughts of being scrutinized flooded my consciousness, but never to the point I felt I needed to flee. I decided to ride it out, I guess you could say. I was determined to see what all the hype of enjoying one's own company was about. As the time passed and I ate my meal, it hit me. There were no expectations. I was able to sit and enjoy the sounds of everyday life without the obligation to say a word. The best way to describe it is by saying this: being by yourself is a chance to decompress. This was the beginning of my acceptance that having alone time to do things I enjoy was not meant to be anxiety inducing, but a time to relax and reflect.

GOING FORWARD

Possibly the most valuable life lesson one could ever learn is everyone has their own story. I don't believe I am the only one who has experienced such traumatic and nightmarish situations and circumstances, nor do I claim my story to be the worst among them. However, I do understand the magnitude of shame and victimization that comes with abuse. There is no man-made vaccination to create an immunization to such atrocities. Each person has a choice: will they be a victim or an overcomer? Making such a decision is difficult in its own right. But making it without the knowledge and guidance of the Holy Spirit makes it much harder to forgive and allow true healing. Some people will spend years, decades, a lifetime even, trying to seek peace and fulfillment and never achieve it. That is the sad reality of a fallen world.

My story could have remained a sad statistic of the ever-growing epidemic of sexual misdeeds and domestic violence. Here comes the "But God" again. But God had bigger and better plans for me. His plans are not based on favoritism, pity, bias, prejudice, or any other divisive category. He has plans for us all. We just have to give Him our lives and He will work out the plans.

Better Than I Should Be

I did just that. I admit I have not always allowed God to follow through with His plans, not because of something He has done, but because of some things I failed to do. I thank Him for His grace and mercy, and for not letting me sabotage myself. The fact that I had a relationship with my parents until they both passed away in 2020 and I loved them [and still do] is a true testament of God's love.

With the exception of a few moments of doubt. I am content with my life. Getting to this point did not come easily. Through life's journey I have come to learn this: just because you think your past is no longer an issue and you have learned to "deal with it," God still sees the need for healing. When He reveals to you the need for healing and you decide to surrender completely, I can guarantee this, He whom the Son sets free is free indeed! Freedom never felt so good!

No longer will past wrongs and dysfunctional relationships rule over or have a place in my life. Either those relationships have been or will be restored to healthy levels or they will be removed. Drama and anxiety have no authority over my life. I choose to be happy. I choose joy! This does not mean every day will be perfect; even the most beautiful rose grows among thorns, so will I thrive

GOING FORWARD

in whatever challenges come my way. Each day I will choose to see the beauty in all things and be thankful for life's lessons. Through my experiences and in sharing my story, my hope is that it will bring you hope and healing too.

ACKNOWLEDGMENTS

I want to thank my close friends Kristie Chappell, Kim Johnson, and Ronda Jaskowiak for your constant encouragement and support through the challenges faced in completing this project. Also, thank you to my childhood best friend, Christa Dally, for being the first to read the beginning manuscript and for giving me the courage to continue. You all have blessed my life immensely.

To the friends I've met along the way, thank you for all of your kind words and encouragement to openly share my story.

Thanks to my parents. Despite how dysfunctional our relationships were, there was one thing for certain: the amount of love we shared. God brought us through so much and showed us the beauty of true forgiveness. Not many will agree or even understand that level of forgiveness. All that matters was in the end you both knew Jesus as Lord and Savior. I intend to see you again one day. Love and miss you every day.

To my sister, Adrienne, I hope my story can help you begin your own journey to healing. I'm here for you and your boys. Love you guys.

Better Than I Should Be

And last but not least, thank you to my children, Tanner and Jaci. Words cannot express my love for you. You have been vital to my healing. You've helped give me purpose and a reason to keep fighting. I couldn't ask for a more caring son and daughter. Love you both and I'm so proud of you.

Printed in the USA
CPSIA information can be obtained
at www.ICGtesting.com
LVHW080523290124
770100LV00012B/278